The Cinderella Coin

A Beginner's Guide for
TREASURE HUNTING on the Internet

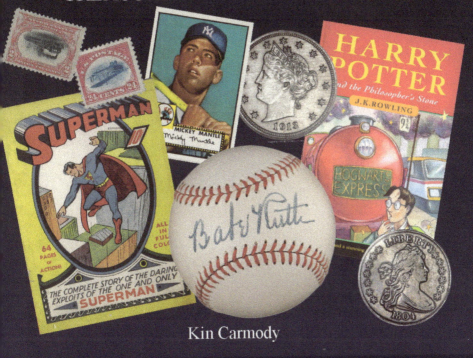

Kin Carmody

Outskirts Press, Inc.
http://www.outskirtspress.com

ISBN: 978-1-4787-9855-2

Cover Design © 2018 Edward K. Carmody. All rights reserved - used with permission. Images courtesy Heritage Auctions Gallery. All interior images used with permission.

Outskirts Press and the "OP" logo are trademarks belonging to Outskirts Press, Inc.

PRINTED IN THE UNITED STATES OF AMERICA

Dedication

This book is dedicated to my daughter Lindsey and my wife Patti, whose stories bring light and humor to my life and to the pages of this book. It's also dedicated to my dear friend Steve Gates, whose courage and perseverance will always be my constant inspiration.

Acknowledgements

My treasure hunt would never have been successful without the support and advice of too many people to completely list, but these few deserve very special mention. HERITAGE AUCTION GALLERIES, who helped educate me in Numismatics and allowed the use of their archival images. DAVID STONE, who was always available for consultation and advice and first brought THE ANDERSON DUPONT 1838-O half dollar to my attention. TAB LEWIS of the National Archives , who went WAY beyond the call of duty to help with my document search.

KEVIN FLYNN and JOHN DANNREUTHER whose research and book "ALIGNMENT OF THE STARS" provided the most comprehensive compilation of information on the 1838-O half dollar ever assembled. R. W. JULIAN, whose historic archival research uncovered the key letters needed to solve the 1838-O mystery. WAYNE HOMREN, who's support was invaluable in publishing my 1838-O research in E-Sylum.

Table of Contents

Introduction

THE CINDERELLA COIN is a true story about an internet treasure hunt. The story is exaggerated in parts for humorous effect, but all the events and actions in the actual treasure hunt took place as described and in the order described.

This hunt began as a challenge, a bit like "Around the World In 80 Days," but in this case the challenge was to find a valuable treasure without ever leaving home to any significant degree. There would be no diving in shark infested waters or slogging through snake filled jungles. The technological world has changed so much in the last twenty years, that now virtually all the searching can be done on the internet and by phone. Vast amounts of information that used to require years of archival search all over the world are becoming instantly available at home, and this trend is accelerating. Just as important, all those "treasures" that used to be hidden away in great Aunt Ethel's attic are now being sold in online auctions. There's no longer any need to dig through the musty contents of boxes that have been stored away for years. All that work is being done for you, so all you need to do is explore the auction sites.

You, the reader, will become part of my treasure hunting team, and you'll follow the successes and failures just as I did.

If I can do it, ANYONE can do it! At the end of this book, you'll learn that there is just ONE secret to success. If you do this one thing and do it well, you too will be able to find your hidden treasure through the Internet.

Part 1
Internet Treasure Hunting 101

Today it's possible for anyone to become a SUCCESSFUL treasure hunter, because both the treasures and the information needed to find them are now on the internet. I made a bet with a good friend that I could do this, be successful, and actually find a treasure of extraordinary value. YOU will be part of my team and learn as I learn, and in the end, you'll be fully able to conduct your own successful treasure hunt.

1

Mondays with Morris

"MILLIONS! EVEN BILLIONS of dollars of treasure just waiting to be found!" I put extra emphasis on "Billions" to try to get Morris' attention. "It's everywhere! You practically trip over it."

It's our usual Monday 5:15 early dinner at the Oakridge Pub. Morris is sitting next to me at our favorite round table next to the fireplace. Its low warming glow casts a flickering light across the table top. Our wives, Patti and Laura, are talking. This is always the way it is after 40 years of marriage. Our wives talk about "wife stuff" while the husbands talk about golf and MAYBE the weather, if it's interfering with "golf stuff." Men at The Landings ALWAYS talk about golf. It's either that or stare at one another all evening in total silence. This puts me at a real disadvantage since I've never actually touched a golf club. The Landings has 6 golf courses, and I've never set foot on a single one.

"How about that 16th hole?" Someone would say. What does that even mean?

When we first arrived at The Landings 10 years ago, I had retired from Australia. It might as well've been from the moon. I would have answered "What hole? Where? Is it dangerous? Maybe we should fill it in before someone gets hurt!" Now, I just nod knowingly and say "Yeah...that ol' 16th hole!" I can't even ask for directions because they're always given in terms of golf holes.

"Oh, we live right on the Marshwood 9th. You can't miss it!"
REALLY? Want to bet?

Morris and I both worked in Hong Kong before I was transferred to Melbourne, Australia. He, for Kodak, and I for Kraft General Foods. We were both "expats" and both lived at Parkview, a huge complex that housed foreigners and looked like a giant red brick fortress on the top of a mountain. Someone must have bribed someone because it was built in the middle of Tai Tam Reservoir Park, and there were no other buildings anywhere near it. I'm not completely sure, but I don't think it's normal to build an apartment complex in the middle of a reservoir. It was all very strange given how crowded Hong Kong is!

Morris was head of Finance for Kodak, Hong Kong, and we became good couple friends. We both retired directly from Asia and ended up here at The Landings in Savannah by sheer coincidence. Patti and I would always arrive first at the Pub on Monday to get our favorite table by the fireplace. When Morris and Laura arrived about 10 minutes later, I would always stand up, give HER a hug and say "How are you?" to Morris. This is universally recognized as an invitation to recite the day's disasters and triumphs on the golf course. Fortunately, Morris knows that he might as well discuss his game with the fireplace, so he's always mercifully short. Morris sat down on this particular Monday and instantly moved to his second favorite topic...INVESTMENTS!

This is HIS area, and I listen attentively as he reels off his favorite stocks and bonds in mind numbing technical detail, and with unbounded enthusiasm. When Morris gets wound up on investments, it's better than a hole in one. As good as HE is, the best financial advice I ever heard came from Laura. I once asked her how she liked retirement, and she said "Humpff! Half the income and twice the husband!"

Morris doesn't know it, but he has an uncanny resemblance to Marty Lagina, one of the two brothers hunting for buried treasure on Oak Island. It's a TV show on The History Channel called "The Curse Of Oak Island." Every show STARTS with a big disappointment like the 2000 year old Roman sword they found last week, which turned out to be part of an old Ford bumper, or the pirate treasure chest which turned out to be a styrofoam beer cooler. Every show ENDS with the treasure hunting team on the verge of an earth shattering discovery. I love the show because I feel like I'm part of the team. I sit in front of the TV when Marty and Rick have their weekly "war room" planning meeting, and I vote along with them. "NO, NO! Don't dig there! Stay out of the swamp! There's nothing there but leeches, snakes and snapping turtles!"

Now that's MY kind of investment! I just know Morris would appreciate Oak Island much more if he only knew how much he looks like Marty Lagina! For some utterly incomprehensible reason, he's more interested in "yield curves" and "REITS," whatever they are, so I'm on a mission to make him see the treasure hunting light.

"Just look at Oak Island." I say "They wouldn't have dug all those tunnels and booby trapped the entire island unless they buried some fabulous treasure....worth billions, maybe even TRILLIONS!" This time I emphasize "TRILLIONS," because the word "billions" just bounced off him last time without even making a dent. I continue with my pitch.

"God knows, they weren't just a bunch of gophers digging tunnels for the fun of it. Even gophers don't dig holes 180 feet deep and then booby trap them!"

The expression on Morris' face doesn't change in the slightest, so I'm guessing he's not quite convinced by my flawless logic. He STILL prefers his REITS...whatever they still are...over treasure that's just waiting to be shoveled into the trunk of his car. I decide to press my advantage. A few more examples should do the trick!

"What about Indiana Jones and The Raiders of the Lost Ark? He's always finding huge treasures like solid gold statues! The secret is just knowing where to look."

Morris thinks about it, but he's not sold yet.

"Most everyone gets killed, and Indiana Jones never ends up with anything. Besides, it's just a movie and REITS are REAL!"

I have to agree to a point. That kind of treasure hunting is expensive, exhausting and dangerous. Who wants to spend their lives wandering around the desert hoping to trip over a gold nugget the size of a basketball, when you'd be much more likely to trip over a nest of scorpions!

Morris does all his own investing and research while sitting in the comfort of his study, and he's very good at it. Now THAT'S the way treasure hunting should be done!

I decide to shift tactics.

"What about The Antiques Roadshow? They find valuable stuff all the time right under everyone's noses? Did you see the one where a lady brought in a really awful painting of the Titanic?"

"No." says Morris unenthusiastically.

"The experts studied it and said the painting was totally worthless, but guess what?"

"I can't even imagine!" Morris says with just the tiniest hint of sarcasm. "Please DO go on."

"They found an actual menu from the day the Titanic hit the iceberg hidden in the back. It's gotta be worth a half a million! Can you believe it? These kinds of treasures are everywhere, if you just know where to look."

Morris STILL appears unconvinced in spite of the overwhelming evidence.

"They only show the good stuff on TV otherwise nobody would watch. 99% of the things people bring in is just junk." Morris adds "I've been studying the yield curve on a California wine company. You really should take a look at it. Now that's a REAL treasure!"

Thirty years ago, I walked into a consignment shop called "The Silk Purse" in Ridgefield Connecticut. In the front window, there was an old 19th century oil painting on display. It was 3 1/2 feet long and 2 feet wide and in an elaborate antique gold frame. The painting was of a whaling ship sinking in a storm, and the crew was in lifeboats rowing away from their sinking ship. The captain was standing in his lifeboat and saluting the ship as it was going down.

I was captivated by the scene and the realistic way the

sea and sky were painted. It was unsigned , but the gold frame alone screamed "priceless!" After some hesitation, I scraped together the $75 price tag and took it home to hang over the fireplace mantel in our living room. I believed that some day I'd discover the artist, because I knew I'd recognize the special way he painted the ocean and the sky.

Twenty years went by, and I never saw anything that looked even close. I even carried a photo of the painting with me to show in antique and art stores. Then one day I happened to turn on The Antiques Roadshow, and THERE it was! It was the very same sea and sky, and that painting was unsigned too! The Antiques Roadshow expert said that the painting was by James Buttersworth, and it was the most valuable single item anyone had ever brought in.

Shortly after, we had an Antiques dealer come to our house to look at some old chairs and rugs, and we asked *him to look at the painting while he was there. He carefully studied the delicate brush strokes, the beautifully balanced composition, the artist's awe inspiring and masterful use of light on the raging ocean and the overhanging storm clouds. He was able to capture both the beauty and the priceless value of my Buttersworth in a single word.*

"JUNK!" He said.

Obviously he was wrong, and I should have checked out his professional credentials much more carefully. I decided not to press the issue of authentication for a couple of very practical reasons. First, I love looking at the painting. It's amazing! The ship still seems to be sinking no matter where you stand in the room.

Once the painting is authenticated, I'd have to store it in a temperature controlled vault, and I'd have to get a special pass just to go visit it. Second, if I didn't put it in a vault, I'd have to get insurance, and believe me, insurance on a million dollar painting isn't cheap! Third, I'd never have a good night's sleep again for fear that an army of burglars was lining up outside just waiting for me to doze off.

Now, this is a most important moment in this story ! It's time to introduce you, the reader, to "Schrödinger's Cat." If you look up Schrödinger's Cat on the Internet, you'll find the following:

Irwin Schrödinger was an Austrian Physicist who studied the behavior of subatomic particles according to the principles of quantum physics. He developed a "story" to help explain his theory, and that story is called "Schrödinger's Cat." Schrödinger's cat is kept in a sealed box with a vial of poison and a radioactive item. If radioactivity from the item strikes the vial, it will break and the cat will die. When you open the sealed box, the cat will either be dead or alive. But, in quantum physics, as long as the box is sealed, Schrödinger's cat is

BOTH alive and dead at the same time! The cat occupies both opposite states at the same time. If you've ever watched "The Big Bang Theory," you'd know that Schrödinger's cat is Sheldon's favorite imaginary pet. I don't like the story very much because I'd never put my cat in a box with poison in the first place. A better way to think about it is to imagine a sealed box with one lottery ticket inside. It's either a winner or a loser, but the drawing is only made the instant the box is opened. As long as the box is sealed, the ticket has the potential to be either a winner OR a loser. It occupies both opposite states at the same time. Anyway, my painting is just like Schrödinger's cat. It's both a priceless Buttersworth masterpiece and "JUNK" at the same time. That dual state will continue until I open the box by having it evaluated by experts. Right now, I have half a Buttersworth hanging in my living room, and it's worth half of a whole lot.

Now that's my kind of treasure hunting! No diving in shark infested waters! No following unreadable maps through rattlesnake infested deserts! Just treasure hunting from the comfort of your own home on the internet. I don't know why I'm the first one to ever come up with this brilliant idea!

"You're so naive about stuff like this!" Morris says. "The chances of picking a winning lottery ticket are better than discovering a lost menu from the Titanic."

His comment about the lottery ticket reminds me of Schrödinger's cat, but I sense from his subtle body language that he may think I 'm a bit naive. He's SO WRONG! I have real world experience in this kind of treasure hunting and the scars to prove it.

My wife Patti is from rural Georgia, and in 1937 her Grandfather won a promotional contest run by Sinclair Oil company. First prize was a box of 12 Babe Ruth autographed baseballs. He hid them high up on the top shelf of his closet and covered them with a stack of old sweaters for safe keeping. They were completely safe from every possible hazard except his two grade school sons. They discovered the box of balls and took one out for a sandlot game with their friends. On one hot sunny afternoon one of the boys hit a home run, and the ball sailed into the town creek. After as much celebrating as any 12 year old boy can tolerate, the boys went home to make another "withdrawal" so their game could continue. These "withdrawals" continued for several years until their father checked out his prized collection, only to discover that there was just one ball left. That one was in perfect condition with a clean, clear, Babe Ruth signature. The ball was immediately put into a witness protection program and relocated to a safe deposit box at the local bank. A perfect Babe Ruth autographed baseball is worth a lot. A beat up ball is still quite valuable, but as interesting as the family story may be, a lost Babe Ruth ball is worth nothing at all!

Patti's father inherited the ball in 1972, and Patti's brother Bill inherited it in 2004 when her father passed away. Last year Bill came to me and said that he wanted to sell the ball because he had no sons and could use the money . I told him I'd help, but it was impossible to get a decent price unless he could prove that Babe Ruth's signature was real. I checked out recent auction results on the internet and estimated that his ball was worth between $5,000 and $10,000. It would have been much more valuable if it had been a home run game ball, but it had never been used in any game. On the plus side, the signature was very clear and sharp, and it seemed to match Ruth's signature on genuine balls. With the family story, I was sure it was real. The story was history, which can be called "PROVENANCE." I learned from The Antiques Roadshow that anything with "PROVENANCE" is automatically worth twice as much as the very same thing without "PROVENANCE." It's most unfortunate that my Buttersworth *has no provenance, but this isn't the kind of thing you can just make up on the spur of the moment.*

The auction site showed that the recognized leader in authenticating baseball signatures is a company called PSA in California. Bill and I agreed that the first step in selling his ball would be to send it to PSA for authentication and grading, and I told Bill that it would be my Christmas present to him.

The day after Thanksgiving, we both went to the post office to mail the ball, and the whole deal plus insurance cost more than $400. PSA has a sliding cost scale for baseball signatures. It's a very long slide, and Babe Ruth's name is at the top of that slide.

The package came back from PSA three weeks later, and we agreed to open it on Christmas Day.

The big day came, and Bill opened the box while I opened and read the enclosed letter.

Now I know what a "secretarial" signature is. It's not exactly a forgery, but it sure isn't Babe Ruth's signature either. It's sort of a legal forgery.

"MERRY CHRISTMAS BILL!"

I wish I'd thought of Schrödinger's cat before opening that box!

With my "BABE RUTH" fiasco still in my mind, I continue my assault on Morris.

"I KNOW I can do it! I KNOW I can find a treasure on the internet." I'll BET you a DINNER I can find a treasure! It'll take some time, but I know it's out there just waiting for me!"

Morris smiles and puts out his hand "You've got a BET," and we shake hands to seal the deal. The treasure hunt is ON!

2

The Comic Book Treasure Trove!

MY MONDAY NIGHT dinner with Morris and Laura has stiffened my resolve. I'm going to find some of this treasure that's just lying around, and I'm going to do it at home through the Internet. A BET is a BET, and I'd prove all those wine sipping, REIT loving skeptics (who ever HE might be) wrong or die trying! I'd just have to be smart about it, AND there's no real time limit, so technically I CAN'T lose unless I DO die trying.

The first step in any good treasure hunt is to decide WHAT to look for. Once that's done, it's a whole lot easier to move on to step 2... which is WHERE to look. This is a MOST excellent start! I can feel myself getting smarter by the minute. This is going to be a breeze!

WHAT to hunt? What to hunt? This is a most important first step because if I decide to hunt for unicorns, I'd run into some problems almost immediately. While it's obvious to everyone that a unicorn would be extremely valuable, it's also very well known that there aren't many around, so I wouldn't be very likely to find one. Step 2 would be a problem too, because I wouldn't have a clue where to begin looking. On the other hand, if I decide to hunt for bottle caps, I'd almost certainly find some, but I might have a hard time selling them, because they're not all that valuable. An old bottle cap isn't a real treasure, if you know what I mean.

I need to find some middle ground.

The bottle cap example may seem a little far fetched, but it really isn't. I have a bunch of old comic books up in the attic that I bought when I was a kid. They just got moved around from place to place and were never thrown away. One of them is a Disney story about UNCLE SCROOGE, whose nerves go to pieces every time someone asks him for money. He has to take a bottle of nerve medicine to stop his entire body from shaking like a vibrating jackhammer. In the comic, his shaking is so bad that the picture of him is just a blur. His doctor tells him that his only hope is to go someplace where no one has ever heard of money, so he can rest. That place is the lost utopian kingdom of Tralla La.

Tralla La is hidden somewhere deep in a secret valley high in the Himalayan mountains, and the people who live there are Asian looking ducks. Scrooge and his nephews all set off to find this lost kingdom. While flying over the Himalayas, Huey, Dewey and Louie tell Scrooge how much this adventure will cost, and he has another panic attack. He opens and drinks a bottle of his medicine and tosses the bottle cap out the plane window. The discarded cap is shown tumbling from the plane into the remote mist covered valleys below. Not to make too much of a point of it, but I never quite figured out why the plane windows were open at 30,000 feet, not to mention the whole issue of littering ! Why not just put it in a wastebasket, or just toss it on the floor like everyone else? Oh well , I'm digressing . Back to the story. The ducks eventually locate Tralla La and parachute into the lost kingdom. It's even better than all the tales and legends. Everyone has everything they will ever need or want, so there's no need for money. Even better still, the ducks are welcomed into Tralla La with open arms, so they settle into their new and perfect life and plan to stay forever.

One day one of the local villagers, in a sampan hat of course, shows up on Scrooge's doorstep.

He's found the old bottle cap that was tossed from the plane in his rice paddy. He's sure it must belong to Scrooge, because he's never seen such a strange trinket before. He's come to return it, but Scrooge tells him to keep it, since it's just an old bottle cap. The villager goes away clutching his new prize, and soon all of Tralla La is consumed by news of the bottle cap. They've never seen such a thing, and it keeps changing hands at an ever higher price. It's value in SHEEP, PIGS and RICE skyrockets! It seems to me that "sheep," "pigs" and "rice" must be the real money in this supposedly "moneyless" kingdom, but I'm digressing again. Finally, the last besieged owner tries to fend off a huge crowd of rabid buyers by telling them "the pride of owning the only bottle cap in Tralla La is worth more to me than FOOD!"

One of the villagers notices the bottle caps on Scrooge's nerve medicine, quickly counts them, and announces that Scrooge is "the RICHEST duck in all Tralla La." Scrooge starts shaking again and has to pop open a bottle to calm his nerves. A riot follows as everyone tries to get the cap as it flies into the crowd.

In order to restore happiness to the happy kingdom of Tralla La, Scrooge realizes he has to make his bottle caps "common" instead of "rare," so he orders his planes to dump ONE BILLION caps into the valley. The first plane load of one million caps is dropped, and peace returns. Every villager is carrying around a bushel basket filled with caps trying to sell them, but no one wants any more...even for free!

Unfortunately, his billion bottle cap order means that there will be 999 more plane loads being dumped on the happy ducks of Tralla La. The planes will fly day and night for weeks, sort of like the bombing of Germany at the end of WWII. Scrooge and his nephews are only spared lynching because they promise to hike out of the valley, stop the bombing and never return.

This book is a "MUST READ" for anyone interested in hunting for valuable collectibles!

There are all kinds of lessons here, but the most important one is that prices and value rise exponentially when there's ONLY ONE of something that more than one person wants.

The second important lesson is that prices collapse, if there is A LOT of something that NO ONE wants.

At this very exact moment, I'm struck by a thunderbolt of genius (beyond the two insightful lessons above). My treasure is right under my nose, or to be more precise, right over my nose and stored up in my attic. It's my incredibly valuable hoard of ancient comic books! Stacks of them in boxes, just waiting to be sold for astronomical prices!

I can see rabid collectors fighting one another for my books, with the price in sheep going up by the second! Enough sitting! I'm ready to spring into action.

I bound up the stairs two at a time and throw open the attic door. NOT such a good idea! It's 2pm on a very hot mid September day in Savannah, where it can be hot at midnight in December. Our attic isn't air conditioned, and the blast of heat knocks me back two steps. It's like sticking my head into a furnace. Thank goodness it's not July or August! Clearly there's a message here. I'm being way too impulsive by simply rushing upstairs without thinking. I need to be more deliberate, more calculating and less "spur of the moment." As I back down the stairs, I realize that my priceless treasures deserve my undistracted attention, and that might be best given at 6 am tomorrow morning when the attic would be a tad cooler.

The next morning I get up at the crack of 9:37am. I feel especially good that I'd managed to curb my impulsiveness to start any earlier. After all, a good nights sleep is ABSOLUTELY ESSENTIAL for sound decision making. The thought does cross my mind that storing my treasures at 120+ degrees for the past 50 years may not have been ideal, but in February it did occasionally drop to 35 degrees and sometimes even lower. I do a quick calculation in my head and figure that the AVERAGE temperature COULD occasionally be about 78, and that's exactly where I set my air conditioning thermostat. Excellent! And what's more, my comics have been protected from the damaging effects of sunlight for all these years by being up in the attic. Smart... unplanned, but very smart!

I go up the stairs one at a time and reach the attic door. From now on it's all about being deliberate AND smart! I place my palm against the door to feel the temperature and make sure it's safe to open. I know this is the right thing to do, because I've seen what happens in movies when you don't do that. Not good, not good at all! The door seems safe, so I crack it a bit and peer inside. NO WORRIES! I'm safely inside and the comic books are in eight large cardboard boxes in the far corner. I quickly, but not impulsively, pick out one box and carry it downstairs. I'd been in the attic for less than 30 seconds and my shirt is already soaked. It was also very hard to breath up there, but I'd heard that a lack of oxygen could be a good thing when storing old papers and books, so I put that down as another "plus."

With the box securely in the trunk of my car, I'm off to visit a local comic book shop, which would be my first step before contacting all the world famous international auction houses! I need to know what I've got.

The comic book store is located in a strip mall on Montgomery Crossroad, and I pull in and park right by the front door. I wrap my arms around the box, especially the bottom, so it won't collapse and dump my treasures all over the pavement. The shop door chimes as I enter. I've never been in a comic book store before, and the sight is STUNNING! The walls are covered from floor to ceiling with racks, and each rack is filled with comic books. There have to be hundreds of racks and at least 30 comics in every one, and the books are all brand new! It seems that each rack is for the latest issue of a particular title, so the comics in any one rack are all the same. In the center of the store are two long cabinets that stretch the whole length of the shop, and the cabinet tops are lined with cardboard boxes. Every one of these boxes is filled with comics in plastic sleeves, and every foot or so there's a yellow divider with an index card separating groups of comics. There seem to be even more comics inside the cabinets, but the sliding doors are shut and locked so I can't see for sure! I've never seen so many comics in all my life!

The shop's empty save for a well dressed older man standing be-hind the far counter at the end of the store. He's slightly balding and wearing wire rim spectacles, and he looks up as I stagger in lugging my box. I take him to be the shop's owner.

"This is VERY ENCOURAGING!" I think, as I look around. The com-ics all seem new, without anything in sight being even a year old, AND there are lots of each one. They have to be as common as bottle caps. The horrible thought occurs to me that the shop owner might try to pay me in sheep or rice for my comics, but then I remember I'm in Savannah and not some far away mythical kingdom. The owner looks promising too! I had expected a young scruffy twenty something nerd dressed in torn jeans and a ty die t-shirt, but this man is obviously a seasoned comic book expert with a vast wealth of experience.

"I've definitely come to the right place." I say to myself under my breath.

The owner watches me struggle in with my box. My two arms are wrapped underneath, and I'm clutching it close to my chest while using my chin as extra support to keep the comics from sliding off the top.

"May I help you?" he says, as I approach his counter.

I'm already greatly impressed! His very greeting cuts right to the chase! Here is a TRUE professional!

"Yes, indeed! I want to get a quick, yet highly professional evaluation of these EXTREMELY rare comic books." I say, as I drop the box with a "thud" on the counter right in front of him.

"Some of THESE are as old as 1944, and the NEWEST is only 1955. That's more than 50 years old for the very newest one!" I pointedly look around at the walls, which hold his vast display of BRAND NEW comics. "I'm the original owner of each and every one, so they all have excellent PROVENANCE."

I emphasize the word "provenance." This is another master stroke on my part, because I know from The Antiques Roadshow that having "provenance" automatically doubles the value of everything. I'm certain that none of the books hanging on his walls have any provenance whatsoever, and a shop like this badly needs some kind of whatever provenance it can get.

The shop owner looks in my box without actually touching any of the comics. Then he moves his spectacles with both hands to the end of his nose, tilts his head and looks at me.

"You're NOT a collector, are you?" It sounds more like a statement than a question.

"No" I respond, with the distinct impression he's evaluating me much more closely than any of my priceless books.

" I didn't think so. Do you have any superheroes in there?" He asks, as he nods toward my box.

"Super what?"

"Superhero comic books, like Superman."

"No."

"Like Batman?"

"No."

"Like Spider-Man, Ironman, The Hulk?"

"No, No and No."

"Any Marvel comics?"

"No, but I DO have a lot of Bugs Bunny, Woody Woodpecker, Andy Panda and Tom and Jerry comics" I say with boundless pride in my voice. "AND, they have excellent PROVENANCE!"

"So you say, and I'm sure you've stored these in your attic where the temperature routinely goes over 100 degrees, and where there are lots of mice and insects." he added.

I was ready for this thanks to my advance preparation.

"Yes, but the AVERAGE temperature is only about 78, AND no mice or insects could possibly survive in my attic during the summer. Besides, there's nothing for them to eat up there."

He gives me a funny look which seems to move from distain to pity, and he reaches into the box for the first time and takes out the top comic. Its spine and cover are perforated with tiny holes as if someone had used it as a dart board.

"Nothing to eat except these!" he says, and he holds the book up as if displaying it to all the customers milling about in his shop, but his shop's still empty.

"Let me tell you something about collectible comic books. Just because they're old doesn't mean they're valuable. People have to WANT to collect them. There are lots of people who collect Superman and Batman, but almost no one collects Andy Panda or Woody

Woodpecker. And another thing, FIRST is always better than just being OLD, like the first appearance of Spider-Man."

"So, how much do you think they're worth?" I ask, interrupting his tutorial.

He ignores my question and continues on.

"The other thing is CONDITION. Condition is EVERYTHING to collectors. Comic books are graded on a scale of 0.5, which is poor, to 10.0, which is perfect or "mint" condition. At the higher grades, the value of a book can DOUBLE when it goes up a single grade point. Because the grade is so important, collectors really want them certified by a respected grading company, so the grade isn't open to debate. Once the comic is graded and certified, it's put in a sealed plastic container that can't be opened."

My eyes are suddenly opened, and a lightbulb goes on.

"Ah Hah! This is just like Bill's baseball. Who knew!"

The shop owner looks at me. "Bill who?"

"Not important. Just thinking out loud. So, what's the condition of MY books?" I ask.

He reaches into the box again. This time he takes out the top 5 and actually opens one. Several loose pages flutter out and float to the floor. I feverishly gather the precious fallen pages to prevent any damage and to make sure he puts them back where they belong. I'm beginning to have some doubts about him.

"They appear to be in ALMOST poor condition," he says, as he turns each one over looking at the front and back covers.

"Well," I reply "At least they're not in POOR condition."

"Actually, that's NOT the way it works. ALMOST poor means they're WORSE than poor, not better! I'd grade them at minus 1.0."

I'm a bit taken aback by his assessment.

"Minus 1.0! That's WORSE than If I didn't have any comics at all! I thought you said the scale went from PLUS 0.5 to PLUS 10.0!" I say in a miffed tone.

"Yes. Yes I did. BUT in THIS case I'm making an exception, because I think they might actually be toxic."

Now I'm getting a bit annoyed.

"OK! So how much?" I say.

He looks into the box again, looks at me, and says "Twenty dollars."

"For the ENTIRE BOX?"

"Yes. I'd have to CHARGE more for getting rid of them if the box was any bigger, but fortunately I know someone in the medical waste disposal business."

I leave the shop WITH my box and feeling somewhat insulted, and I return them to their cozy home in my attic. I do a quick scan for mouse droppings when I finally put the box down. I don't see any, casting more doubt in my mind about the legitimacy of that dealer. I wonder what kind of condition he'd be in after 70 plus years locked up in my attic with nothing but comic books to eat!

I suspect he may be related to the guy who looked at my Buttersworth. Now that I think about it, I'm sure there's a family resemblance. His brother, most likely. It's 1pm and it's getting a mite "stuffy" in the attic, so I quickly retreat downstairs.

Patti loves the musical group The Pink Martinis. They have about 13 musicians and a lead singer named China Forbes. They sing in dozens of different languages, so It's a very upscale show. Once each year, the Pink Martinis perform at The Melody Tent in Hyannis on Cape Cod. We had never been to The Melody Tent or seen the group perform in person, so a couple of years ago I bought tickets. It was on a Saturday evening in mid August, and it was unbearably hot outside with the temperature well above 90 all day.

The Melody Tent is HUGE and can seat several thousand people, but it's still a Tent, and it isn't air conditioned. The center stage, where the musicians play, rotates slowly so everyone in the audience gets to see the same views throughout the course of the performance. We arrived at about 6:30pm at The Melody Tent parking lot. Warily, I asked the parking attendant what it was like inside the tent. He looked at me through my open car window and said "TOASTY!"

The performance began, and the stage lights clicked on. While it was hot outside, it was even hotter inside, and the hottest place of all was on the stage under all the lights.

The leader of The Pink Martini's began by introducing the different musicians in the group, when he suddenly stopped in mid sentence. He looked up at the lights and then down at the rotating platform.

"You know..." he said. "I feel like a rotisserie chicken!"

I make a mental note to move my comic books once the temperature in the attic drops below "toasty."

3

Phony Baloney

THERE'S A PROBLEM! I first stumbled on it with Bill's baseball, but now I can see it everywhere.

When I was just a kid, one of my most favorite things to do in the whole world was to visit Ephram's book store in Worcester. It was half way down a major street that bordered a park in the center of the city. Ephram's mostly sold books, which were of less than no interest to me whatsoever, but they also had lots of old used comics in back which they sold two for a nickel. This was smack in the middle of my budget. Granted, toward the high end, but still in my budget. I'd come into the shop, go straight to the back, and spend about 10 minutes going through the comics to see if any different ones had come in. Usually there were one or two, and they'd set me back a whole nickel!

That was good, but that's not why I loved to go into Ephram's. As soon as you walked into his store, you were confronted by two all glass display cases side by side. Both cases had rows of long metal trays stacked one on top of another, and the trays would rotate inside the cases so you could see what was in each one. The cases were locked, and there were two buttons on the lower right corner of each. Press the top button, and the rotation would stop so you could look at all the things in the top tray. Press the bottom button, and the rotation would start again until there was another tray filled with things you wanted to see. It was like a miniature ferris wheel going round and round, and It would "click" every time one of the trays moved into the top position. It was very hypnotic. I'm sure my mother came in looking for me many times and found me in front of one of Ephram's magic cases in a complete and total trance. As I said, the cases were locked so you could LOOK but NEVER touch. This was especially true if you were under the age of ten, and your total budget was just 5 cents. If you happened to have real money (which I never did), and you wanted to see something up close and actually hold it, you had to go get Mr. Ephram. He'd come over and unlock the case with lots of grand flourishes and gestures. I guess he did this to impress upon everyone who was watching just how valuable all the things in his case were. He would hover over you until whatever you were looking at was safely back in his locked case. I was always hanging around, looking at the things in the cases, and leaning in as close as possible to see anything that was taken out of his rotating treasure vaults. I think I may have annoyed Mr. Ephram when I got between him and his customers, so I could get a really good look at whatever priceless object he'd taken out. When I did this, which was almost ALWAYS, the customer would usually bend down and show me what he was looking at. Sometimes, he'd actually let me hold it to look for myself. Mr Ephram seemed to be on the verge of a combined stroke AND heart attack whenever THAT happened.

By now, you MUST be wondering what was in those trays that was so captivating. Every tray was filled with old coins and stamps that were unlike anything I'd ever seen before! Each item was in a rectangular white cardboard holder with a cellophane window, and they were all lined up next to each other so none overlapped. There were no spaces between them, but I could see everything. There were hundreds in all the trays, and everyone was different. It was a wonderland of bizarre and strange things from long ago. There were 2 cent pieces and 3 cent pieces! Who EVER heard of such things? There were real GOLD coins, some as big as a silver dollar ! There were dollar bills with pictures of Indians and bison on them, and they were HUGE! THREE TIMES as big as the dollar bills my mother had. All of these marvels were a wonder to see, and every rotating tray brought even more. BUT, there was one thing that was truly fantabulous to behold! Despite the never ending parade of miracles, I'd always freeze the rotating tray when THIS one item came up, and I would stare at it endlessly. I couldn't take my eyes off it! It was an old 2 cent stamp, with a red border and a black train in an oval in the middle. The train was all black, and there was black smoke pouring from its smokestack as it roared down the black train tracks. The train was UPSIDE-DOWN! The smoke was UPSIDE-DOWN! Even the tracks were UPSIDE-DOWN! This was WAY beyond impossible to believe! The white holder had "1901 two cent invert" written at the bottom, and that meant that the train had been accidentally printed upside down when the stamp was made. The price was written at the top of the holder...$5,000! CAN YOU EVEN BELIEVE! That was more money than I'd ever heard anyone say in all my life, but even that fantastical price seemed way too low for such a miraculous object!

image courtesy of Heritage Auction Galleries

Year after year I'd come into Ephram's just to look at his amazing stamp. I worried that some billionaire might buy it despite the astronomical price, but it was always there in its slot right in the middle of the top tray. Everything was as it should be, until one dark day when I was eleven. I was standing at the case, hypnotically staring at the most important single thing that the universe had ever produced, when I noticed something a bit odd. The edge of the oval that had the picture of the upside down train was starting to lift up from the rest of the stamp. I peered much closer. HORROR UPON UNSPEAKABLE HORROR!

The edge had lifted up just enough so I could see the edge of a right side up train underneath! I raised my hand to cover my mouth, but I couldn't stop my gasp of shock and disbelief. The center was merely a cut out from another one of those stamps, turned upside down and then glued in place. My beloved treasure was...WHAT? Can I even SPEAK the word?

A FRAUD? A mere sales gimmick designed to hypnotize and torture little boys? All of the above?

Many years later, when I was working in Asia, I made one of my frequent trips to our Philippine company in Manila, and Ed Puno was our Philippine company President. In one of our social conversations , he mentioned that he had bought some old U.S. silver dollars in his travels in South East Asia. I said that I'd be interested in seeing them, and he brought them into his office the next day. They were in one of those old blue folding albums with holes made especially for dollars. I opened the folder with some degree of curiosity, interested to see what Ed had picked up. I looked at the first dollar and asked him if I could take it out of the album, and he nodded in agreement . I asked if I could do the same with the second, and he said "Go ahead." I looked at both together side by side. They were silver dollars alright and VERY old. Then I turned to him and said;

"May I give you some advice?"

"Yes?"

"Don't try to sell these both at the same time to the same person."

"And I shouldn't do that because?" he asked.

"Because they're both dated 1804, and 1804 silver dollars sell for more than $3 million apiece. Your buyer probably wouldn't have enough money for both...at least not in his pockets at that moment."

Of course they were counterfeit, and Ed knew that. He wanted to see if I knew. After my traumatic train episode, I wasn't about to be fooled again, except for Bill's baseball. So here's the problem. The more valuable something is, the more likely it is to be phony.

If you find an ordinary 2 cent stamp, the chances are 99.999% that it's real.

If you find a 2 cents stamp with an upside down train, the chances are 99.999% that it's a phony.

This makes it a bit difficult to find rare collectibles that are both VALUABLE TREASURES and REAL at the same time.

The Treasure Target

SO, MY VENTURE into rare comic books was a bit of a bust. No matter! I was getting smarter even if it was just an inch at a time, and I learned several valuable lessons.

First, just because something is old doesn't mean it's valuable.

Second, just because something is rare doesn't mean it's valuable. Collectors have to want it.

Third, rarity AND quality are both important.

Fourth, being first is always good.

Fifth, make sure what you're looking at is REAL.

Sixth, Don't look for treasures in you're own attic.

Seventh, and maybe most important of all, I need to know more about my target than anyone else. When I went into that Comic shop, I should have known more about my comics than anyone else in the world. More than other collectors, more than the shop owner and more than all the experts. That's the only way to see things that others miss. Knowledge is EVERYTHING, and it can be picked up at home on the internet.

In 1717 the pirate ship Whydah was wrecked in a storm off Wellfleet, Cape Cod.

The Whydah was carrying gold and silver when it went

down, and it was never recovered until Barry Clifford found the wreck in 1984.

I've walked our beach for years, always hoping to come across an old pirate coin washed up from the deep, but no luck! Even though I've never found one, I might, because I know what one looks like. Silver coins corrode in the salt water, and after 300 years a pile of coins buried in sand at the bottom of the ocean looks like a pile of fused charcoal briquettes. Most people don't know that and would actually walk around them because they look dirty.

You have to KNOW what to look for. This is true for pirate treasure, and it's true for every other kind of treasure as well.

After my comic book fiasco, it's high time to decide on a specific treasure target. Whatever it is, I want it to have a big collecting base and rare items that fetch exorbidant prices...lots and lots of sheep! These categories all fit the bill. It isn't even close to a complete list, but it's a good start.

Antique early American furniture
Paintings
Other kinds of art (e.g. "folk")
Jewelry and gemstones
American coins
American stamps
Comic books
Baseball cards
Sports memorabilia
Antique toys
Posters
Pottery and Glassware
Old/ first edition books
Historic artifacts
Real Estate

Each of these categories might work better for some people than for others depending on their interest and experience. For me, there were only two that made sense now that Comic books were off my list...coins and stamps. This may surprise you readers, who probably think that "fine art," especially oil paintings, would be my obvious selection because of my stunning success with my Buttersworth. The truth is that I don't have any confidence at all when it comes to art. My Buttersworth is a fluke, pure and simple. When it comes to art, I feel like a 5th grade boy at his first dance. I 'd much rather be in class studying geography, and I HATE geography. Geography is the WORST! After all, you ARE where you ARE, so what on earth is the point of studying where you aren't? Anyway, I had a terrible artistic trauma in first grade.

Everyone in my class was making a painting, and mine drew the attention of my art teacher right away . It was a GIRAFFE, and it had spots and even horns that were just the right length. It had exactly the right shaped head and a long giraffe tongue sticking out. My teacher said how wonderful it was over and over again! When she left to look at the other paintings, I finished it up just like any proud budding 6 year old artist would do. I added two sets of wings and painted it blue and yellow, except for the wings, which seemed to demand electric orange. When she came back, she told me I'd ruined it. Then there was the whole "finger painting" thing. Who wants to stick their hands into buckets of different colored axel grease, and then try to clean them off on big pieces of white paper hanging on an easel? If we could have done the same thing but cleaned our hands off on our classmates instead, I might be an artist today!

So art was out and so was furniture because of my uncanny ability to break everything I sat in, including all my grade school chairs. They really aren't built for any kind of twisting, and jumping from one to another doesn't work at all!

Stamps and coins are the most logical choices for me because of the endless hours of brainwashing I had at the hands of Mr. Ephram's rotating hypnotizer. I also know a little bit about collecting pennies. I had one of those blue cardboard penny albums, and collecting pennies was WELL within my 5 cent weekly budget.

I got my Lincoln penny albums for Christmas when I was nine. There were two of them. The first went from 1909 to 1939, and there were 3 circular slots for each date. One slot was for pennies made in Philadelphia and those didn't have a mintmark letter under the date. I called them"plain." The second slot was for SanFrancisco ("S") minted pennies and the third for Denver ("D"). The second album went from 1940 up to 1956, but it had a whole bunch of empty unmarked holes that could be used for future years. That Christmas, I went through everyone's loose change, and they gave me all the pennies I needed to fill the open holes. It was no big deal! I didn't really think about it much, because I liked my comic books much more than the pennies. Over the next two years things started to change. My second album became completely full except for one huge hole in the last page for something called a "55 double strike." What's more, most of my pennies were from recent years, so they were shiny copper rather than dull brown, and I liked the shiny pennies much more than the brown ones. I decided every penny in my album that wasn't bright and shiny had to be replaced as quickly as possible! Now, I was looking through loose change for bright new looking replacements for ones I already had. If the album was full and all the pennies were glowing, my collection would be complete, and I desperately wanted it to be complete. Of course, that was only possible with the new album, because it was impossible to find bright, new looking pennies older than 1940. And there was STILL that pesky

*blank hole in the middle of my new penny album. The 55
double strike was an error like the upside down train stamp.
Its date and all the lettering on the front were stamped twice
over each other causing them to be doubled.*

Image courtesy of Heritage Auction Galleries

*It was very rare and impossible to buy, especially on my
budget of 5 cents a week. My only options were to find one
or live with the empty space. THAT was when I first discovered BANKS! I don't think I'd ever been in a bank before, but
now I went with my mother once every week. When she was*

finished with the teller, I'd step up and hand her a $5 bill and ask for ten rolls of pennies. The five dollars was my entire Christmas haul, but I wasn't spending it. I'd take the pennies home, sort through them, and then re roll them for the next week. Ten rolls is 500 pennies all at once! That's more than a whole year of loose change from all my relatives all at once!

Things started to change. I was becoming a TRUE collector. My mother would walk into my room and I'd be lying on the floor with a pile of 500 pennies in front of me. I'd look at each date and then put it into one of two other piles. There was a "forget it" pile and a "maybe" pile. Over the next hour, the big pile would shrink away to nothing and the "forget it" pile would have all the pennies except a few. I'd replace the ones I wanted to keep, and then I'd re roll all ten rolls and write my name on each one. I had to do that just in case I miscounted, and one of my returned rolls didn't have EXACTLY 50 pennies. I was VERY careful and counted each roll three times, because I knew that my welcome mat at the bank window would be withdrawn forever if any of my rolls turned out to be short. One day in 5th grade, I found my missing 55 double strike. I instantly knew what it was like to have the only bottle cap in all of Tralla La. I brought it into school and showed EVERYONE, whether they cared or not! Then, I carefully placed my long missing treasure into its empty slot, and at last the album was full. BUT, something was wrong. Something was VERY, VERY wrong!

My 55 double strike was BROWN, while all the other pennies around it were bright and shiny like new. This wasn't good! My collection looked better WITHOUT the 55 double strike than it ever did with it. Also, some of the ones before 1950 weren't new looking either!

This story doesn't have a happy ending. I knew I'd never find another one, let alone one that was brand new, and it was impossible to buy. I did the only thing left to do. I traded *in my $5 search fund, bought a bottle of liquid copper clean-er and cleaned every single penny until they all looked new. NO, new isn't exactly the right word. Until they all looked "WHITE." The tarnish was all removed and my pennies were all shiny white, so at least they all looked the same. All of a sudden, I completely lost interest in my pennies. I took them up to the attic, where they are today, and I came back down with an armload of my favorite Woody Woodpecker comic books.*

Using copper cleaner on a penny collection is a bit like using scotch tape and a magic marker to "fix" my Buttersworth. It's not quite as bad as trying to clean my painting with steel wool, but it's pretty close. Collectors view repaired and cleaned things like they've contracted Ebola. I've decided that RARE AMERICAN COINS will be my treasure target, but I sure as heck won't clean any of them this time!

5

You Have to Buy Your Treasure on the Internet

YOU, THE READER, have probably figured this out by now, but if not, it's time to tell you.

You remember at the very beginning when I told you about "The Curse Of Oak Island?"

I said then, that one of the reasons I liked the show so much was because I felt like I was on their treasure hunting team. Well, from this point on, YOU are on MY treasure hunting team, and you'll discover what I discover exactly when I discover it. You'll be with me for each decision I make and every step of the way. Just like "Oak Island," you'll be able to say "Don't do that, don't look there!" And, just like "Oak Island," I'll do it anyway, but you'll have the satisfaction of saying. "See! I was right! You should've followed my advice." It's also very likely that you'll see some of the answers BEFORE I do. That's good too, because it's proof that you'd be better at this than I am.

On January 5, 2013, the treasure hunt actually begins. That night I'm watching the national news at home in Savannah. One of those "human interest" stories comes on. It's about an old 1794 silver dollar. It's supposed to be the very first (first is always good!) silver dollar made at the U.S. Mint. It had sold at auction the day before for 10 MILLION DOLLARS. A 1794 silver dollar is rare, but it's not all that rare.

There are about 150 in existence. Granted, this one was in nearly perfect condition, but the price was so high, because it was believed to be the very first.

At that moment, I know that my treasure target will be rare coins, because if I can find the right coin, it can be worth a fortune! Now, that you know WHAT we're hunting for, I need to tell what's actually going through my mind, as I think about how I'd go about doing this. In truth, I'm having some awful thoughts about what COULD happen IF I FOUND a whole bunch of coins (like a treasure chest in my back yard), or IF I BOUGHT some really valuable coins at dirt cheap prices.

WHAT IF I FOUND A TREASURE CHEST IN MY BACK YARD?

I spend a lot of time working on my flower garden at our beach house in Cape Cod. We're right on the ocean, and there really isn't any good dirt for Hydrangeas or Rhododendrons. I have to dig holes at least 3 feet deep and then fill them up with good dirt, so I can plant my shrubs. I've been doing this for years, and I've always had the dream that one day my shovel would hit something hard. Oh No! Not ANOTHER rock! But it isn't a rock. It's the top of an old metal chest! I dig up the chest without too much trouble because it's only about two feet long, a foot wide and a foot deep, but Boy Howdy is it ever HEAVY! I can only move it side to side, until it's finally out of the hole. It's all rusted, but I pry open the top with a big screwdriver and open it. It's filled with Spanish gold coins and must be part of Black Sam Bellamy's treasure from the Whydah. One of two things can happen.

The first thing that can happen is...

This is SO exciting that I wrestle and haul the chest into my house, and then I call the local newspaper and the national TV networks. They arrive, and there are news trucks parked all over my precious flowers and shrubs, but no worries! I can buy enough new ones to completely cover my new house, my new swimming pool and my new 6 car garage, which happens to be filled with my 6 new cars. That night my treasure find is all over the news! The calls from family and friends begin as soon as the TV segment is over. They all congratulate me, and they all end by saying that we MUST get together much more often, and shouldn't be such strangers. After that, the phone rings every five minutes with calls from people I've never met or heard of before. Everyone of these strangers has a heart wrenching tale that makes me cry! I disconnect my home phone and put it my garage along with all the cell phones just in case they can still ring even though they're all turned off.

The next morning, I still can't believe my good fortune, when there's a knock on my front door. I open it, and there's ONE man in a dark suit with a brief case. He tells me he's from the state of Massachusetts, and he has a court order that I can't dispose of any of the treasure, because it's all state property. He leaves. Ten minutes later there's another knock on my door. I open it, and there are TWO men in dark suits, and THEY tell me I can't dispose of any of the treasure. It all belongs to the Federal Government, because I live near the beach, and that's all National Seashore property. Ten minutes later, there's a knock on my door, and there are THREE men in dark suits. They tell me they are from the National Historical Preservation Trust, and I can't dispose of any of the treasure because they're required to put it all in a museum in Washington. They see the pried open chest, and tell me to not touch any of this ever again, because I might do further damage to "the people's property" and I could go to jail. They also tell me my house will have to be vacated and torn down , because the entire area is now a NATIONAL HISTORIC SITE. Ten minutes later there is another knock at my door. I open It, and there are FOUR men in dark suits. They hand me their business cards, and tell me that they're lawyers and will represent me for a small fortune, payable in advance.

The second thing that can happen is...

I am NOT so excited that I do anything rash, like tell any living, breathing soul what I've found, and that includes Patti. I drag the treasure chest inside, and hide it in the basement storage closet where no one (Patti) ever goes. Next, I rush out to the local garden store and buy a nice BIG hydrangea, which I plant in the treasure hole. I spread out lots of wood chips and dead leaves, so it looks like it's been there for years. I don't want anyone coming out to the house, noticing my

rectangular treasure chest shaped hole, and start asking questions...
now, or later, or EVER! I need to think HOW to sell my treasure without
attracting any unwanted attention? A single coin at a time seems the
best way to avoid having all the men in dark suits knocking on my door.
Well, just like Bill's baseball, it's impossible to sell even a single coin
without having it certified. I start with just one coin and send it off for
certification. This is a test, but it doesn't go as well as I'd hoped. I get a
call from the certification company.

"Yes?"

"This is 'Honest Abe's' certification company, and we just received
your coin."

"Yes?"

"And we'd like to know a little more about it before we certify it."

"Yes?"

"It appears to be genuine, but where did it you get it? We need
to know its background. Who owned it before you, and where did it
come from?"

(silence on my part while thinking.)

"Well, actually, I found it on the beach...can you believe it?"

"Reeeeaaally!" he says, his voice dripping with skepticism. "How
very implausibly lucky of you! You DO understand that we can't certify
anything that might be stolen, not that YOURS is stolen, of course."

Ten minutes later there is a knock on the door. I open it, but this
time there are TWO men in police uniforms and just ONE in a dark suit.

"I know who YOU are, nodding at the two policemen, but WHO
are you?"

"I'm from the IRS!" The man in the suit answers enthusiastically.

Even if I did manage to get away with it on one gold coin, can you
begin to imagine trying to do this 2,000 times?

You can see from my daydream, that the only sane option here
would be to haul the treasure chest back to where I found it, rebury it
and plant my hydrangea back on top.

Now, I imagine the second possibility...

That I'm able to buy REALLY RARE COINS AT DIRT CHEAP PRICES

FROM SOMEONE'S INHERITED COLLECTION.

I decide that there are lots of very rare coins hiding among the inherited things that've been passed down for generations without being given a second look. These are the kinds of things that people bring to The Antiques Roadshow, and that's where they discover their true value. I place an ad in the paper that says I evaluate and buy old coins. My ad is VERY successful, and the phone rings off the hook. I have ten potential customers on the very first day! Once again, One of two things can happen.

The first thing is that can happen is...

A young man comes to my house with a 20 pound bag of old coins he got from his grandfather. After three hours of looking at every single one, there's nothing worth anything more than the silver melt value of the coins. They're old worn dimes and quarters his grandfather saved when he was running his corner liquor store. I do NOT want to buy his 20 pound bag, and the young man is not happy.

A young lady comes in with another 20 pound bag, and after another three hours the results are the same. She is not happy, and I do NOT want to buy her bag either.

Fifty other people come in over the next month, and none of them are happy, and I don't want to buy any of their bags. This is not turning out to be a good business model, and all my ex customers are saying lots of bad things about me. THIS is where those billions of old coins went. They were all put into grandfather's bureau drawer. Seventy years later, they were put into bags, and every one of them was brought to MY house. If this keeps up, we'll probably have to move.

The second thing that can happen is...

One day, after a year of pouring through bags of worthless old coins, an elderly lady comes in on a walker with an album that was passed down to her by her grandfather.

She says "My beloved grampa Jim gave me this, and asked me to treasure it always. I've kept my word for 70 years, but now I have no money, and my 17 cats are starving. Tomorrow, the bank will foreclose on the house grampa Jim built with his own two arthritic hands.

They're going to tear it down, so they can build an Adult Bookstore, and we'll all be put out on the street to search through garbage pails for scraps (Mind you, her cats have absolutely no problem with this!). I open it up the album, and it has a number of very valuable coins with a total auction value of more than a million dollars.

"Now, this is killing me here," I say, "but I COULD give you as much as $100 for this musty, dirty, old album filled with useless old metal that no one wants...JUST as a very special favor to you and your adorable cats."

SERIOUSLY? This is wrong on so many levels, I have trouble even writing it. Why not skip the middleman altogether and just rob a bank? Granted, their coins aren't rare, but I could make up for it in quantity.

Most of the stuff that's brought into "The Roadshow" has been in someone's family for years. BUT, occasionally, you see something that goes like this.

"WOW! Worth a MILLION BUCKS you say! And to think I just bought it for 25 cents last week at Sid Jones' yard sale! That's Sidney P. Jones, at 223 Grove Street in Indianapolis." How long do you think it will be before Sid finds out? I'd bet Sid gets a half a dozen phone calls before that show is even over.

"Hey there Sid, you'll NEVER guess what I'm watching on TV right this very second!" And WHAT ABOUT Sid? Do you REALLY think he'll say "Boy, that guy sure was LUCKY buying it from me for only 25 cents! Good for him!"

So here's my conclusion from my two daydreams. I CAN'T sell rare coins that I've found in a treasure chest, and I CAN'T steal them from people who don't know what they're worth. The only thing left to do is to buy rare coins at auctions and on line, and try to get the lowest possible price. I'll have to buy rare coins that have a much greater value than the owners, bidders or auctioneers realize. This would be true for paintings, stamps and for everything else too. THIS is where your internet research comes in! Your research will make it possible for you to see great value where others don't. KNOWLEDGE is the single most important key to success in treasure hunting on the internet.

6

What's Hot and What's Not

NOW THAT I'VE decided to buy VERY RARE coins at VERY LOW prices at auction, I have to figure out what auction house to use, and what coins to bid on. It seems to me that my biggest advantage is that I'm not a compulsive collector, who'll pay any price to fill that last pesky hole in my album. I can bid low, and if I lose, so what! I'll just bid low on something else.

The auction house question is an important one, and the best answer depends on your comfort and risk level. Every conceivable collectible, including coins, is sold on EBAY. Many of the eBay items are "certified" by recognized third party graders, so that can eliminate some risk, but many other items are sold "as is." These can be very difficult to return, if you change your mind, or if you don't feel the item is 100% as listed. Many sellers put things on eBay at VERY HIGH asking prices just hoping to get lucky, and some listings are extremely high just to get noticed as a form of advertising. The major advantage with eBay, or any other lesser known site where individuals sell directly to a large potential audience, is that the seller may not know, or fully appreciate, the true value of the item being sold. This CAN happen, especially if YOU are the first person to identify and recognize a particularly rare variety of an item. It wasn't very long ago that minor differences in coins caused by different die pairs used for striking were not factors in valuation or rarity. Today, those extremely rare die varieties can be worth a fortune! If you were the first to recognize a rare die variety, you could scan all the auction listings and just purchase the rare variety at a regular price. The more YOU are the world's expert on a particular item, the more potential opportunity there is for you on these individual seller sites.

The nature of collecting is evolving in ALL categories, but some categories haven't caught up quite yet. There are lots of on-line auction websites. Some cover lots of different categories like Heritage, E Bay and Hake's, while others are very category specific, like Comic link. You'll need to search the web to find the sites that best meet your interests and needs.

Comic books are a good example of a relatively "under-evolved" category. The highest prices are being paid for certain well known issues, like Superman and Batman. With those key titles, the first issue is ALWAYS valued at a much higher price than later issues, and the higher the quality, the higher the price. The status of owning the first Superman comic is like owning the only bottle cap in all of Tralla La. However, there are large numbers of issues and titles that are much, much rarer than Superman #1 or Batman #1, with very few copies made and very few known. At some point, it's likely that the hobby will start to value these extremely rare issues more than it does today, but that hasn't happened yet. The safest, and probably best, choice for many rare collectibles is HERITAGE AUCTION GALLERIES. HERITAGE is the world's largest coin auctioneer, and they have auctions every week. They have really big auctions every 3 months, and that's where the rarest and most expensive coins are bought and sold. They also have experts you can talk to before buying anything. No lawyers, Government officials or police knocking at my door...unless I don't pay my bill, but I have a sneaking suspicion they won't send me anything until AFTER I pay. STACKS BOWERS is another superb rare coins auction house, but their auctions tend to be less frequent than those of HERITAGE. I decide to start my treasure hunt with HERITAGE.

With that settled, the fun part begins, and that's to decide WHAT to buy. I don't know much about rare coins, so the first thing to do is to order and read a coin price guide book. I order The Red Book coin price guide from Amazon and begin reading as soon as it arrives. Have you ever sat down for a pleasant relaxing afternoon and opened up a good exciting old fashioned telephone book, and just started reading? That's what reading coin guide books is like. I think they're supposed to be used to look things up, rather than read cover to cover for pure entertainment. There's no plot, no story and endless columns of numbers. At least a telephone book has names. On the plus side, RedBook has lots of pictures, and there aren't any pictures in the White Pages whatsoever! In addition to what old coins look like, here's what I learned.

First, modern coins are NOT rare! I came to this stunning insight all by myself by reading the number of coins made in recent years and by looking at the prices, which are rarely more than the cost of a burger and fries. Just take pennies for example. In 2013, the US mint made 7 Billion pennies! That's like 7,000 airplane loads of a million bottle caps each to be dumped on the happy people of Tralla La. Instead of carrying around one bushel basket of bottle caps, each happy villager would have to carry around 7,000 baskets! I suspect the entire valley would be filled to the top, like a giant wastebasket.

Second, the best way to tell if a coin is rare is to look at the prices. High price equals rare. Low price equals NOT rare.

Third, I DID learn something a bit less obvious. There are two kinds of coins people collect. The most popular by far are coins that were actually made to be used by people to buy things. These coins are made for "circulation," and I call them "real coins." It's the money we spend every day. The other kind are PROOF coins, and these are made just for collectors. There are far fewer of these Proof coins than coins made for circulation. They're made in a different way, so they have sharper details, and their surfaces can be like a mirror. Because there are so many more collectors of circulation coins, in many cases they can cost more than proofs for the same year, even though a much smaller number of proofs were made.

In rare cases, the US mint only made proof coins for collectors, but didn't make any for circulation. if you want that date in your collection, you don't have any choice. Those are called "proof only" issues and are always very rare, because so few were made in total.

I learned one other important thing. Now that I'm an expert, I shouldn't be calling these folks "coin collectors." I have to call them "NUMISMATISTS." I guess it's like going to the "orthodontist" instead of going to the dentist.

With my home schooling in rare coins nearly complete, I'm ready to learn about the REALLY rare coins that sell for a couple of million each, not that I have anywhere near THAT kind of money to spend. The whole purpose of this treasure hunt is to SELL one for a million dollars, not to BUY one for a million dollars, but it can't hurt just in case! After all this IS a treasure hunt.

I go on line and look up the rarest, the most important and the most valuable coins ever made. I find out that these three things aren't always the same. Here is MY list of the top five U.S. coins.

1. The best quality 1794 Silver dollar. The FIRST silver dollar made (about 150 known in all conditions). Sold for 10 million dollars.
2. 1933 20 dollar gold piece. Sold for 10 million dollars (only one is legal to own).
3. 1804 silver dollar. 16 known specimens (all proof). Sells for between 3 and 5 million dollars.
4. 1913 Liberty nickel. 5 known specimens (all proof). Sells for between 3 and 5 million dollars.
5. 1894 - S (SanFrancisco minted) dime. 24 minted (all proof). Sells for about 2 million dollars.

There are a whole lot of rare coins that sell for more than a million dollars, but these five are all very famous, so owning one is a real "status" statement. It's like owning the Hope Diamond, a Picasso painting or the only bottle cap in Tralla La.

THE 1794 SILVER DOLLAR

There are about 150 examples, and many are in pretty rough shape. Buying a well worn 1794 silver dollar is expensive, but still affordable. It's possible to buy one for between 100 thousand and 150 thousand dollars. Owning one is a status symbol, because it's the FIRST dollar made, and because the making of this first dollar is an interesting story. However, the really high prices in the millions are only paid for those few in the very best condition. This is a REAL coin that was actually made for circulation. If I could FIND one of these in top condition, it would be like finding a real treasure!

Courtesy of Heritage Auction Galleries

THE 1933 TWENTY DOLLAR GOLD PIECE

In 1933, the U.S. minted almost HALF A MILLION twenty dollar gold pieces. That's a lot of coins, so how could they possibly be rare, let alone worth ten million dollars?

In 1933, President Roosevelt took the U.S. off the "gold standard," which meant that the Federal Government no longer had to give you gold in exchange for other money. He also ordered the melting of all the gold coins on hand. Since none of the 1933 twenty dollar gold pieces were ever released into circulation, they were all melted. All, except about 10 which were stolen before the melting took place, so these coins are very rare, but they're also totally illegal to own. They're sort of like a stolen Rembrandt. How the heck can you ever sell one! However, there is ONE that IS legal to own, because the Federal Government issued an export license when the coin was sold to King Farouk of Egypt. When Farouk's collection was sold, the 1933 gold piece came up for auction, and the Feds sued to recover it as stolen property. They lost their case, because in issuing the export license, they basically said the coin was Legal to own. THIS is the coin that sold for 10 million dollars, but the others are still illegal to own or sell.

THE 1804 SILVER DOLLAR

There are 16 known examples, but this is a very peculiar coin. For many years, no one knew when, where, or even why it was made, and its mystery is the reason it became so famous. Now we know that a small number of proof 1804 dollars were made in 1834 as part of proof sets given to foreign dignitaries. More proofs were made in the 1850's through the 1870's for important collectors. The 1804 Silver dollar is NOT A REAL COIN by my definition. The few that were made in 1834 were authorized, but were never meant for circulation. The production of all the others were proofs made for collectors. All that doesn't matter because it's so famous, and owning one is such a status symbol. All specimens are well known and accounted for. They're so famous that there's no chance one of these would ever show up on my treasure hunt list. There are also thousands of fakes, so IF I did happen to find one, it wouldn't be real.

Imaged by Heritage Auctions, HA.com

Courtesy of Heritage Auction Galleries

THE 1913 LIBERTY NICKEL

The 1913 Liberty nickel is flat out NOT a legitimate coin, aside from having been produced at the Philadelphia Mint. It's production was never authorized, and it was made in secret for some important "collector." As the story goes, once this guy had his hands on the five proof (not made for circulation) nickels, he advertised far and wide that there were rumors that a few 1913 Liberty nickels had been minted. He offered to pay $500 for one, and the story spread like wildfire! Soon, the entire country was looking through their loose change to try and find a 1913 Liberty Nickel. After a couple of years, with no finders and with the bounty going up, he announced that he had five. He was was willing to sell them for a small fortune, which he did. This whole thing seems to be a fraud from beginning to end, BUT that minor point hasn't kept these coins from routinely selling for more than $3 million today. All 5 are accounted for, so finding a 1913 Liberty nickel isn't a realistic treasure hunt option either.

Imaged by Heritage Auctions, HA.com

Courtesy of Heritage Auction Galleries

THE 1894-S BARBER DIME

This is another highly questionable coin. Before 1968, almost all proof coins were made in Philadelphia. There are a few rare exceptions, when some unauthorized branch mint proofs were made. There is ONE case in 1855 where authorized proofs were made in SanFrancisco to honor the start up of silver coin production at their new mint.

It seems that a couple of well placed SanFrancisco Mint employees got together in 1894 to produce 24 proof dimes in secret. The 24 proof mintage number was included in the official San Francisco mint report, but it was never officially authorized. It's said that these employees divided up the 24 dimes among themselves and saved them as future rarities. Even though these coins were "manufactured rarities," they knew that their value would skyrocket over the years.

As the story goes, a young girl named Hallie Dagget was given 3 of these dimes by her father and told to tuck them safely away, because they'd be very valuable some day. "Some day" can be a very long time away, especially since THAT particular day was unbearably hot! Hallie went into Macy's and bought herself a nice cool refreshing bowl of strawberry ice cream, which was her very favorite! Truly a dime well spent in her humble opinion. When her dime was found in change, it created another sensation, and everyone started looking through their dimes in addition to their nickels. That coin is very famous and is now called (not surprisingly) "The Ice cream parlor dime."

Despite the fact that 1894-S Barber dimes are "not real" coins made for circulation, they still sell for about 2 million dollars.

Courtesy Heritage Auction Galleries

All these extremely valuable coins have a couple of things in common. Most importantly, very few exist of each, and they all have AMAZING STORIES! Their rarity, coupled with their stories, make them all Numismatic status symbols. That means collectors would love to own any one of them, EVEN IF they didn't happen to collect that particular type of coin. It's the same as "the pride of owning the only bottle cap in all of Tralla La." The status of owning one of these coins far outweighs the fact that they may not even be "real," authorized, or even legal. Owning one is more important than food. So here is another important lesson. A STORY greatly adds to the intrigue, mystery and desirability of an item. The better the story, the more valuable the item. Just think about THIS. How much would it cost you to buy a set of used 60 year old golf clubs? NOW, how much would it cost if those same clubs had belonged to JFK? See my point? Your research can uncover a hidden story just as easily as identifying a rare previously unknown variety.

7

The Hunt Begins

THE VERY NEXT day, I call Heritage Auction Galleries," The World's Largest Numismatic Auctioneer," and I am connected to a coin expert named Ed.

"This is Ed."

"Hi, my name is Kin Carmody, and I want to buy a very rare coin."

"Really! That's excellent! You've certainly come to the right place! May I be so bold as to ask exactly what coin you want to buy?"

I wasn't ready for that question, mostly because I didn't know the answer.

"I don't know yet, but it has to be rare, with fewer than 20 made, and it needs to have a VERY good story, and it would be VERY nice if it were REAL!"

"REAL?" Now, Ed's tone was a bit less enthusiastic. "We here at Heritage DO NOT sell counterfeit coins! It tends to be quite bad for business, especially with our repeat customers."

I try to start over and get back in Ed's good graces, after all I am a potential customer, and I badly need his help.

"I'm sorry. I didn't mean 'not real' as in 'counterfeit'. I meant 'not real' as in not made for circulation. I'd like to buy a coin that was actually made to be used by people to buy things, rather than just made as a 'proof' for collectors...but that's NOT absolutely essential." I quickly added.

"Have you ever bought anything with us before?" he asks.

"No."

"I didn't think so." Ed responds.

Suddenly I felt I was being teleported back to the comic book shop, and it was "deja vu all over again." I need to let Ed know I was a serious customer...and QUICKLY!

"I want to buy something REALLY rare at a VERY LOW price!" After I say it, I have a sinking feeling that I haven't made things all that much better with Ed.

"Don't we all." Ed says dryly, but then he adds "Heritage has weekly auctions with all kinds of excellent coins. They're ALL graded and certified by the major grading companies, so there's absolutely NO risk to you as to the quality or authenticity of a single one. We stand by EVERY sale!"

Now THAT sounds good!

"You can bid on line at our website, and place any bid you want no matter how low, as long as it's higher than the current highest bid. For example, if you were the very first bidder on an 1804 dollar, you'd automatically be high bidder, even if you only bid one dollar. You'd stay high bidder until someone else outbids you."

No risk! That sounds even better.

Ed continues with his his bidding lesson. "While it's extremely unlikely, you might even win with a very low bid. It DOES happen, and this would allow you to place the kind of bid you're comfortable with, and who knows? You might get lucky!"

That sounds PERFECT, and I wouldn't even have to leave my chair either!

"May I make a suggestion?" Ed offers.

"Please do!"

"Once every 3 months or so, Heritage holds a big auction, and these auctions are where the very rarest coins are usually sold. We put out a detailed full color catalogue of all the auction lots. Actual bidding can be done in person on the auction floor, over the phone through a Heritage representative who is on the floor, OR in advance on our auction website. Internet bidding in our Winter auction will begin tomorrow and will last about 25 days. I think you should check it out, and study the lots for sale."

I thank Ed, and ask if there is any special coin he'd suggest.

"There's an 1895 Morgan dollar I think you'd find interesting. 880 proofs were made, but NO circulation strikes. It's a 'proof only' issue, so there's lots of demand, because so many people collect Morgan dollars. The 1895 Morgan has a good story too! The Philadelphia mint made 12,000 circulation strikes, but they were all melted because of the Pittman act. It's known as "The King of the Morgans.""

"Thanks very much, Ed. I'll look at the '95 Morgan, and if you have any other suggestions, please let me know." I give him my telephone number and email, and he promises to send me the Winter auction catalogue.

"I wonder what The Pittman act is?" I think to myself after hanging up.

I know a little something about Morgan silver dollars. They're called "Morgans," because that's the person who designed the coin. I also know the primary purpose of Morgan dollars was to be put at the very bottom of every Christmas stocking, so It'd be the last surprise you'd take out. I know that, because I have two brothers and one sister, and there was a Morgan silver dollar in the bottom of everyone of our stockings until we were too old to get stockings. I also know that they're the heaviest coin ever made anywhere, anytime and anyplace. I once had two in my pocket at the same time, because my sister was only four and agreed to trade me hers for a dollar bill, because it was too heavy for her to carry around. They don't "jingle" like pennies. They just "clank," and they're so heavy I ended up walking on a slant. I had two in the same pocket, and my mother thought I'd hurt my back because of the way I was walking.

I also know that banks used to be filled with them, because nobody wanted them. Once, when I went in to exchange my ten rolls of pennies, the teller said;

"Wouldn't you rather have five nice shiny new silver dollars instead?" If you had dollar bills, any bank would rush to trade them for their silver dollars, just to make more room in their safe. I tell you, they couldn't give 'em away! All that changed in an instant, when the price of silver went through the roof. Then, people lined up at the teller windows to get all the Morgan's they could carry, and guess what? Suddenly, the banks didn't have any at all...not a single one! All very suspicious, if you ask me.

So, I know a lot about Morgan dollars in general, but I don't know much about an 1895 Morgan. I decide to take Ed's advice, and I click on the Heritage Winter auction site and then click on "Morgan dollars." There's a list of dates from 1878 to 1921, so I click on 1895. There's an 1895 "S" (for San Francisco), 1895 "O" (for New Orleans) and an 1895 no mint mark (for Philadelphia).

I click on the 1895 no mint mark, and THERE'S the coin Ed suggested. It couldn't have been easier! The picture shows the front (obverse) and back (reverse), and both sides are so shiny they're like mirrors! There's a write-up under the picture that tells about the coin, and there's a place to bid, but it says that bidding won't open until tomorrow morning. The write-up is REALLY GOOD, because it tells the history of the coin, and it details any marks or blemishes. It also has a full list of how much other 1895 Morgans have sold for at other Heritage auctions, so it's really easy to tell if you're getting a good deal or not.

The story is just as Ed had told me. Only 12,000 circulation strikes ("real" coins) were made and everyone believed that they were all melted. BUT, no one has ever actually proved that they were all melted, because there aren't any records of melting by date. If someone ever found an 1895 circulation strike that escaped melting, they say it would sell for MORE than 10 million dollars, and it would be one of the most valuable coins in the world! Collectors have been searching for a circulation strike Morgan for years without any luck. This 1895 Morgan didn't have its own special story, but it was graded Proof 64 Cameo. Proof 64 is a high grade, given that grades only go up to 70, and the highest grade ever given to one of these coins is a 6.8. "Cameo" means that the head and eagle stand out from the coin's mirrored background. "Cameo" is better than "not Cameo."

This is pretty darned close to what I was trying to find. Even if this particular coin doesn't have its own story, all 1895 Philadelphia Morgans as a group do, and this is a high quality example. Also, I like looking at the coin, which helps. I've always been a sucker for "shiny." I'll bid on it tomorrow as soon as the bidding opens. I WILL be the very first bidder!

At this point, I need to say one other thing about HERITAGE AUCTION GALLERIES. They auction all kinds of collectibles. They sell comic books, baseball cards, sports memorabilia, jewelry, art and just about anything you can think of. They even have auctions for minerals, gemstones and fossils! Heritage is a great place to get started, no matter what category you choose for your treasure hunt. Even if you never buy anything, you'll get a whole lot smarter about what you're looking for.

8

The Art of the Bid

I'M AT MY desk five minutes before bidding opens. Last night I studied the write- up for the 1895 Morgan dollar. Heritage has a chart that shows their estimated final selling price for every coin in their auction. For the 1895 Morgan, they show a selling price range between $50,000 and $55,000, and that includes their sales commission.

That's a whole lot of money, and you may say "I can't even begin to afford THIS kind of treasure hunting!" That may be true, but you can start off by bidding on things that only cost $100, and try to double or triple your money. Once you get the knack of it, you can build up to more expensive items. With a proven record of success, you could even get someone to "invest" in your bid, provided it doesn't go any higher than a certain amount. I sure would invest in a $100,000 dollar bid on an 1804 Silver dollar. If I didn't win, there's absolutely no cost. If I did win, I'd make a fortune. The amount of the bid really isn't a problem if I bid low enough, because there isn't any risk. I can turn around almost immediately, and resell it for a whole lot more. You probably think that can't possibly happen, but it DOES, and here's why. On these very rare coins, there are only about 5 to 10 active bidders, and the number of bidders can vary auction to auction, even though an identical coin might be for sale. If there are only a few bidders, then the end price usually ends up lower than if there are a lot of bidders.

The idea is to put in a bunch of really low bids on a bunch of different rare coins and hope that one of them only has a few bidders. The price ranges that Heritage shows are based on past sales, so IF I can buy something well below that range, I know I've gotten a great deal! Last night I figured out what my bid would be for the 1895 Morgan. If I bid $40,000, my total cost, including commission, would be about $47,000. I would just break even if I resold it at $47,000 plus commission. That's NOT treasure hunting, so forget that! If I bid $30,000, I'd make $11,000, but if I bid just $20,000, I'll double my money! That's the right place to be, AND it would make for an excellent "I WIN the bet!" dinner, compliments of Morris and his Wine Company!

The "BIDDING IS OPEN!" sign flashes on my laptop. I'm NOT going to mess around. No low ball $1 opening bid for me...I'm in for the full enchilada! My heart is racing, as I place my $20,000 opening maximum bid and click "confirm." Seconds later, there's a "ding" sound, and a beautiful green message appears on my screen.

"CONGRATULATIONS! YOU ARE HIGH BIDDER! YOUR OPENING BID IS $1, AND YOUR MAXIMUM BID IS $20,000." I've NEVER bid so much on anything before, and I'm half exhilarated and half scared to death. I like their green message. It's a very soothing and reassuring color, and I really need a lot of reassuring right now. It also happens to be the color for "full speed ahead," AND it's the color of money! All the other bidders would eat my dust! They could bid $1 or $100 or even $1,000, and they'd get NOTHING, NADA, ZILCH, ZIPPO! The Morgan is mine (so far) with zero risk, and it's all so easy!

This is like running a race! It's only the first day of 25 days of bidding, but I'm already leading the bidding pack.

I can't wait, so I call Morris to tell him the fantastic news!

"I'm THE winning bidder on an extremely rare and important coin! I haven't officially won it yet, but it's pretty much in the bag."

After a short pause, I quickly add;

"My RETURN ON INVESTMENT will be 100% in just 2 months."

Morris really likes "return on investment," but he calls it "R.O.I.," because he's on a first name basis with all kinds of financial terms.

For Morris, having a good "R.O.I." is better than having both good "PROVENANCE" and a hole in one at the same time.

"That IS good news! Please DO keep me posted!"

It's surprisingly hard to tell the difference between skepticism, sarcasm and genuine enthusiasm over the phone, so I decide to go with "enthusiasm."

I go back to my laptop to take another look at my first success, and there it is, in glorious green letters "CONGRATULATIONS! YOU ARE HIGH BIDDER! Your winning bid is $1,000, and your maximum bid is $20,000."

"That's odd!" I think to myself "My winning bid should be $1, NOT $ 1,000."

Suddenly the screen blinks again and my winning bid changes to $2,000. Obviously something is wrong with my laptop, or the Heritage website, or both. No worries! I have 25 days to get it all sorted out.

Two weeks later, I'm sitting at my laptop trying to calculate exactly how much I'm going to make on the resale, when I hear the distinctive "ding" of an coming message. I open it.

"YOU HAVE BEEN OUTBID! THE CURRENT MAXIMUM BID IS $22,000. THE NEXT MINIMUM BID IS $24,000."

This is AWFUL news! This is NOT something I expected. What's worse, the message is in emergency, full stop RED. No soothing, comforting green here! My heart is pounding, and I'm starting to sweat. I had exactly this same panicky feeling two years ago, when we were driving up to Cape Cod from Savannah, and the red "check engine" light suddenly flashed on half way through the trip. Fortunately, that turned out to be just a loose gas cap, but THIS is no gas cap. I desperately want to make that red message go away! I don't really HAVE to double my money in just two months. Maybe I'm being a bit too greedy. I type in a new bid of $24,000, and click on the "confirm" button.

In 5 seconds, there is another "ding," and I anxiously open the new message. Its soothing green words bathe my eyes, and it's curative powers massage my body and restore all harmony to the universe! My heart rate drops back to normal and my sweating stops.

"CONGRATULATIONS! YOU ARE HIGH BIDDER..."

Thank goodness things are back to normal, and all is good with the world!

My state of Zen calmness lasts exactly three minute and fifty seven seconds, when it's interrupted by another "ding!" This ding seems especially urgent. I hope, perhaps, that the earlier message forcing me to raise my bid was just a terrible error on the part of Heritage, and they're sending me a note begging for my forgiveness.

There, right in front of me, is the garish red engine warning light AGAIN! This is beginning to get tiresome. The next bid will have to be at least $28,000. I type in $28,000, but this time I jam down on the confirm button much harder!"

"WELL!" I say out loud to my empty room "THAT should teach them a lesson!"

I have no idea who's on the other end of this unprovoked assault, but I suspect it may be a vast consortium headed up by some unscrupulous Eastern European Oligarch.

"DING!," but instead of green, it was yet another red message. STILL outbid!

It's like that old TV show "Lost in Space," where the robot keeps saying over and over again "WARNING, Will Robinson! WARNING, Will Robinson!"

NOW I'm no longer annoyed, AND I've moved well beyond peeved! I'm MAD!

I enter another bid, this time for $32,000, and I jam down on the confirm button as hard as possible without punching right through the laptop.

"DING!," and the comforting green CONGRATULATIONS message is back where it's supposed to be. I stare aggressively at the laptop screen for fifteen full minutes, just daring it to misbehave again. It's finally learned its lesson. It doesn't make any more unwanted noxious noises, but I'm beginning to believe that there never was a problem with my computer or the website. The problem all along has been some obsessed nutcase collector who doesn't know when to quit.

I do a quick calculation. Bid $ 32,000, add on 20% and that makes $38,400. Let's say I resell at the bottom of the range, I'll STILL make more than $4,000, and that's more than 10% on my investment in just two months.

Not too shabby! I can live with that!

"DING!" the red light goes on.

It probably won't come as much of a surprise to you readers, but I didn't win the auction for the 1895 Morgan dollar. The winning bid was about $55,000, which was at the very top of its estimated sales range. Well, so be it! It was a learning experience, and it didn't cost me a cent! There were probably too many bidders all competing for this one coin, and that drove up the price. I need to try something different. I need to do a test!

The next Heritage weekly auction would begin on Monday, so I pick out 15 different coins, and each one has an estimated sales price of about $1,000. Monday morning, I'll place a $400 bid on every one. THIS will be a test to see what percent of the 15 bids I win.

Monday morning, the bidding opens and I'm ready to go. After I place my 15 bids, my laptop starts to sound like a musical instrument... "Ding! Ding! Ding! Ding!..." It was like the Emerald city in The Wizard of Oz. I was surrounded by a beautiful sea of green congratulations. At the end of the week, I'd see how many of my bids were winners, and that would give me a pretty good idea of my long term batting average. I'd put them up for resale as fast as I bought them. It's all very scientific, and a lot of small coins can add up to one big coin, like the 1895 Morgan.

The auction would be over Sunday night, but late Sunday afternoon my laptop started going crazy. It seemed to be having a nervous breakdown with a torrent of angry "dings," until there were 15 new messages followed by silence. Was it dead?

NO! My sea of green had been replaced by a sea of red. All I could see was an emergency service station with an endless line of cars, with all their red "check engine" lights flashing at the same time.

"Coin collectors are all NUTS, just like the villagers in Tralla La!" I said out loud, and my empty room heartily agreed!

9

Opportunity Calls

I **PLACE A** few more low bids over the next month but never come close to winning. I'm ready to give up and talk to Morris about his wine company, and that's when the phone rings.

"Hi, this is Ed, from Heritage. We talked last month, and I said I'd give you a call if I had something you might be interested in."

"Yes?" At this point both my interest and enthusiasm has evaporated.

"Do you know anything about the 1838 New Orleans minted half dollar?"

"A little," I say stretching the truth a whole lot. I did know that since it was minted in New Orleans, it had to have an "O" mint mark on it somewhere, but that's ALL I know.

"Well, as you undoubtedly know (and of course I didn't because I'd never even heard of it), the 1838-O is considered to be the rarest half dollar ever minted, and in the last half of the 19th century it was believed to be the rarest of all American coins. There are only nine known examples, and one of those is in the Smithsonian museum."

I don't say anything, so Ed just goes on.

"Of course they are extremely expensive, usually selling for more than half a million dollars. I have a client who has one in the lower condition range, and he wants to sell it through a private sale rather than though a public auction. It's RELATIVELY affordable because it's not as high quality as any of the others."

"What exactly is RELATIVELY affordable?" I ask suspiciously.

"The price is three hundred and twenty five thousand including commission."

"DOLLARS?" I gurgled my question in an obviously strangled voice.

"Yes, and I think it's a very fair price. At public auction, it could sell for quite a bit more."

"Is it REAL?" I ask.

This time Ed understood what I meant by "real."

"This coin is graded Proof 45, but it's a "proof only" issue, so there aren't any circulation strikes. THAT makes it as real as an 1895 proof Morgan dollar, AND it has a GREAT story!"

My interest meter, which had been stuck way below zero, twitched up the tiniest bit. After all, I was looking for a story, and my low ball bidding had been a total bust so far. For THAT kind of money, it BETTER have an amazing story!

"So, what's the story?"

Ed goes on, and it's a VERY good story!

"No one really knows WHERE, WHEN or even WHY these half dollars were made. No mint records of their production have ever been found. It's considered to be one of the greatest unsolved mystery in American Numismatics today. Experts have been writing articles, and even books, on the 1838-O half dollar for more than 120 years. There are all kinds of theories, but no one has ever been able to solve the mystery."

The dial on my interest meter actually moves up to zero. Now Ed has my attention.

"There's another very interesting point. In 1894, an 1838-O came up for auction, and it had an old piece of paper wrapped around it. It was a note from the Chief Coiner of the New Orleans Mint. His note said that the coin was a presentation piece, and not more than 20 had ever been made. The note was published in July 1894 and then disappeared, and it's never been seen since. We here at Heritage believe that this coin being offered COULD be the same one that had the famous note wrapped around it."

I'm definitely interested, but I'm still choking on the price.

"There is ONE more thing." Ed added, "In 2012, two of our best researchers published a booklet on the 1838-O half dollar. Why don't I send it to you? It has all their latest information and theories, and you might find it interesting."

"Great! Please DO send it."

Ed finishes by saying that he would need an answer from me in about 10 days, so he could contact other potential buyers if I'm not interested. There's no pressure, but I'd have to make a decision.

The booklet arrives from Ed three days later, and it's titled "The Surprising History of the 1838-O Half Dollar" by David Stone and Mark VanWinkle. Their booklet has pictures of all 9 known coins and next to last is the one for sale. It's called "The Anderson DuPont specimen." They all have names. Apparently, if you happen to be a very rare coin, you get a name. It's a good thing they don't give first names to every coin, otherwise it'd be a nightmare trying to buy anything!

There are a couple of things in the booklet that catch my attention. First, while they BELIEVE the Anderson DuPont specimen is the same one that had the note wrapped around it, that has never been PROVEN. It's just speculation. Second, and most important, Anderson DuPont has some unusual features that none of the other coins have. It has reverse marks that COULD have been made during the minting process. They reprint a letter written by Rufus Tyler, the Chief Coiner of the New Orleans Mint, to the Director of The U.S. Mint. In that letter, Tyler states that he was only able to make 10 half dollars, and then the reverse die collapsed, so he couldn't make any more. The reverse marks on Anderson DuPont MIGHT be consistent with what would happen if the reverse die collapsed. Again, this is just speculation.

Anderson DuPont also has some debris on its surface that looks more like "die rust" than dirt. If the dies that are used to make coins end up rusting, then their surfaces get pitted. These rust pits are depressions that look like tiny reverse bubbles in the dies. Then when the dies are used to strike coins at high pressure, a reverse raised impression of these pits is struck onto the surface of the coin. So die rust isn't really actual rust on the coin. It's just the impression of the rust spots on the die. In "The Surprising History," Stone and Van Winkle believe this possible die rust means that the other eight 1838-O half dollars COULD have been minted as test proofs in Philadelphia and that Anderson DuPont is the ONLY ONE that was actually minted in New Orleans. They believe the dies MIGHT have rusted while in storage in the hot humid climate of New Orleans, and that all other half dollars struck from those same dies should show similar die rust. Since none of the others have this "die rust," then they had to have been made BEFORE the dies rusted and that would have been in Philadelphia.

While this is ALL speculation, there is real evidence to support their theory, and they make a very good case. It's easy to see the material, whatever it is, on the surface of Anderson DuPont, and it looks very different from all the others. Did I mention that the coin itself looks BLACK! I looked at a picture on the Heritage Auction Archives website right after Ed's call, and both sides look black. Mr. Anderson DuPont is blackened to the point where he looks like he's been slow roasted in a fire!

When I turned seven, I was allowed to have my very first birthday party with friends, not just family. It was on July 7, and I was allowed to invite six of my soon to be second grade classmates. My mother planned an afternoon picnic lunch down at our pond, which was across the street, through the woods and a mile away. We were going to have a campfire and cook hotdogs and MARSHMALLOWS! My six guests were dutifully dropped off at our house at about 11 am, and we all trooped across the street and down to the pond. Our campsite was on a knoll, surrounded on three sides by a forest of tall pines. On the last side was the pond, which was filled with frogs, snakes, turtles and all kinds of excellent attractions for a pack of seven year old boys. At the very top of the knoll was a stone lined fire pit with a metal grill. The spot had a beautiful view of the pond, and the pink and white pond-lilies were all in bloom.

My father was an austere man, who once said to me "I prefer to meet my children on the ADULT stage." I didn't realize it at the time, but he really meant "all children." He wasn't very much of a "picnic" kind of father. When he saw the seven of us, he didn't see a birthday party. He saw a WORK PARTY, and he put us all to work hauling brush and logs, and generally cleaning up the woods around the picnic area. After about two hours of this, he realized that even conscripted workers need to be fed, so the fire was lit, and the hotdogs were brought out. Since my former friends were no longer speaking to me, or to each other for that matter, I tossed a few pennies I had in my pocket into the fire one at a time. This way I could avoid looking at any of my unhappy guests, because I was obviously very, very busy. Anyway, the pennies all turned black, just like the 1838-O half dollar, so that's how I know.

IF Stone and VanWinkle are right, then this coin COULD be a really BIG deal! It would make Anderson DuPont the only New Orleans Minted 1838-O half dollar, and that's exactly the kind of thing that would double or even triple its value.

IF Anderson DuPont is the same coin that was found with the note wrapped around it, then it could be traced all the way back to the coiner who made it. That would be extraordinary, because that kind of lineage is virtually unique, and it would also be something that could increase its value. THAT would be PROVENANCE is spades!

Finally, the 1838-O half dollar has an amazing story, and the mystery hasn't been solved yet. Very few people know about the story, and that's something that could increase its value too.

The problem is that these things are all ideas and theories, and ABSOLUTELY NOTHING has been proven. To increase the value of this coin over its very (gasp!) high price, some of these theories would have to be PROVEN, and by that I mean proven to the complete and total satisfaction of all the Numismatic experts. There can't be a shred of doubt, and that kind of "proof" is very hard to come by. Even if I do PROVE something, it's still possible that none of the experts will believe it.

The Anderson DuPont coin was auctioned once before by Heritage in 2008, so there's a good high resolution picture in their archives. I spend the next three days studying the picture and comparing it to the images of other 1838-O half dollars, especially the "Atwater" and the "Eliasberg" specimens. These are the very best pictures available, and I'm able to draw some solid conclusions after a lot of intensive study of the pictures. Stone and Van Winkle could be RIGHT! The Anderson DuPont coin SEEMS different from the others. The material on the surface of the coin looks like die rust and not just dirt. There are marks on the back that certainly look like they were caused by the collapsing reverse die. IF that's true, then THIS COIN was definitely minted in New Orleans, which leaves open the possibility that the others were not. Can I PROVE any of this, and is it worth the very high price to even try? I'm going to have to wrestle with that question up until the very moment I have to call Ed with my decision, but right now I have a couple more questions, so I give him another call.

"Hi Ed, this is Kin. I have a few questions about the half dollar that you might be able to help me with."

"Yes. Sure! If I don't know the answers, I'll call someone who does and I'll get back to you. What are they?" Ed says helpfully.

"The first question is...WHY is it called the ANDERSON DUPONT specimen? Was it named after a famous collector like Eliasberg?"

"I can answer THAT one! This coin has only been traced back to its earliest auction appearance, and that was the Anderson DuPont auction in 1954, so that's the name it's been given."

(I need more!) "Who WAS Anderson DuPont?"

(I get less!) "Anderson AND DuPont were the two lawyers who represented the seller in the '54. Auction."

(I feel like I'm going backward here.) "LAWYERS? Who owned the collection? It MUST have been some famous collector!"

"No one knows. The owner wanted extreme privacy and went to great lengths to make sure his/her/its identity would NEVER be known." (I AM going backwards.)

"So this coin is named after a bunch of...LAWYERS?"

Ed hesitates a bit before answering "...WELL yes, but it WAS a very famous auction, and the auction carried the Anderson DuPont name."

"Ed, if I DO buy the coin, can I CHANGE its name?"

It's funny how you can tell if you've just crossed over some sacred line, even if you're on the phone. I could feel Ed's sense of total disbelief at the audacity and inappropriateness of my question. I might as well have asked if I could change the colors of the American flag to mauve, puce and violet.

"No!" he answered forcefully. "THAT just isn't done! That's NEVER been done!"

I'm not 100% satisfied with Ed's answer

"Why Not?"

"BECAUSE, that's its name !"

"Oh. OK. Thanks!" I'm NOT at all impressed with Ed's logic, but I sense it's best to move on.

"Why is the coin BLACK?"

"No one knows for sure. It was discolored in some way, but we don't believe it was ever cleaned. More importantly, PCGS (the grading company) doesn't mention any cleaning or artificial coloring, and they're the ultimate judge on things like that. If it had been cleaned, they would have flagged it on the holder. They ALWAYS do!"

At least THAT made me feel better. This wouldn't turn out like my Ebola tainted penny collection up in my attic.

"Thanks Ed! I'll get back to you shortly with my decision." And I hang up.

Now THAT was a very interesting conversation. So, it's impossible to change the Anderson DuPont name!

I was born in Worcester Massachusetts and GIVEN the name Edward Kinsley Carmody after my mother's father, Edward Kinsley. He died shortly before I was born, so it was a logical choice. Ed, Eddie, Bud, Ned, are all reasonable nicknames, and EDWARD isn't bad as a formal name. England had more King "Edwards" than just about anything else, except maybe King "Henry." However, this wasn't to be! My mother's only brother was named Edward, and he was called "Eddie," or "Uncle Bud" to me. Unfortunately, back in the 1940's, Worcester was not one of the most socially liberal places on Earth, and my Uncle Bud did something that caused tongues to start wagging well beyond the city limits. Uncle Bud swapped wives with his best friend. This just wasn't done in polite, or even impolite, society in Worcester, and it led to the obvious question "WHAT kind of going-ons were taking place that led to this mutually acceptable trade" My father failed to see the humorous side of "Uncle Bud's" little escapade, so Uncle Bud was banished from our house. This was NOT your usual kind of banishment. THIS was a total ban, which carried with it the banning of his name in addition to his person. The name "Edward" and all of its derivatives were NEVER to be spoken again in the presence of my father. Not even IN the house, when he wasn't even there. Since my first name is Edward, this led to a "naming" crisis. What should I be called? Since I was too little to talk, the problem wasn't a pressing one. Simply pointing at me, or referring to me as "the boy," worked fine until I was about four. My father would say "Boy, come here!" or "Boy, do that!" My mother was a mediating influence, and she pointed out that I had TWO older brothers, who also happened to be boys. That argument didn't fly, because my father didn't call them "boy." They were too old and had REAL ALLOWABLE names. "BOY" was now my REAL name. I liked watching the early Tarzan movies with Tarzan, Jane and "BOY," because it was comforting to know that at least one other kid was named "boy" too! My mother finally won out when I was old enough to go to nursery school. She said it was likely that there'd be at least one other boy in my class of twenty, and "boy" might be a bit too generic for my teacher. She also pointed out that just calling me by my last name "Carmody" wasn't going to work in a family of six, where everyone had the same last name. My father finally gave in, and it was decided by default that I'd be called by my middle name "KINSLEY."

"What is wrong with that?", you may ask. WELL, the problem was, and still is, that "KINSLEY" is almost impossible to pronounce in the United States. It's like "Washington" or "car" in Worcester. Everyone in Worcester wants to take the "R" out of "car" and put it smack into the middle of "Washington," so you have people saying "I'm gonna drive my CA to WARSHINGTON and then I'll be comin' back to WUSTA." Everyone, and I mean EVERYONE except my immediate family, would slot a capital "G" into the middle of my name calling me "KinGsley." So THIS is how it was every single time I went outside with my mother. We would pass by a friend or acquaintance she hadn't seen in some time, and the conversation would go like this.

"OH, Joan! It's SO good to see you! How are you? and THIS (pointing at me) must be your son KinGsley!" All of them would say "KinGsley" like my name was a mountain, and the "G" they put in the middle was the peak, so it needed all kinds of extra emphasis. The first part and the last part of my name was totally unimportant. The only thing that mattered was that the "G" was as strong and clear as possible. The "G" had to "ring" like a bell. My mother would instantly leap to correct this verbal blunder with a fifteen minute lecture on the origin of my name.

"THIS" she said, pointing back at me "is KiNsley!" He's named after my father Edward KINsley. It's an old English *name dating back to the "Doomsday Book"...blah, blah, blah. They tended the King's sheep...blah, baa, baa...baaa ..became. "King's Lea" blah, blah, blah...Came over on the Mayflower and dropped the "G", becoming "KiNsley" blah, blah, blah." THE END!*

And just WHAT would they say after my mother's story? THIS is what they would say every single time without exception!

"Why Joan! What a WONDERFUL story! And every one of them would bend down, look me in the eyes and say "And SO nice to meet you KinGsley!" with the "G" still ringing in my ears.

I was sent off to boarding school when I was twelve, and as soon as I arrived, I was determined to change my name. I liked a bunch of different names especially STEVE and PETER, but I knew they wouldn't work. My parents would come to pick me up for Christmas vacation, and they'd say "We're here to pick up KINSLEY." The dorm master would say "Who? We don't have anyone here by THAT name. Are you sure he's enrolled in THIS school? There are other schools that are close by. Perhaps he's enrolled in one of those."

So very embarrassing, and I could miss Christmas vacation too! The other boys in my class were called "Johny," "Timmy," "Bobby" and the like, so I settled on "Kinney," until I became too old for the "Y" and then I'd be just plain "Kin." It'd be the same as moving from short pants to long pants, like boys did when they grew up a hundred years ago.

SO, it's IMPOSSIBLE to change the name "ANDERSON DUPONT?" Just WATCH me! I may buy the coin JUST so I can change its name!

10

The Mystery of the 1838-O

SINCE YOU'RE NOW part of my team, it's important to give you all the facts and theories about the 1838-O half dollar that we have at this moment. Here's what we know.

When Andrew Jackson became President, one of his top priorities was to encourage and support westward expansion. One of the greatest obstacles to westward expansion was the lack of a reliable money supply, and local banks often issued their own "money." Unfortunately, they went bankrupt at an alarming rate, so Jackson wanted to establish a branch Mint to supply official U.S. minted silver and gold coinage for the West. Before 1838, the only mint was in Philadelphia, and its location was totally inadequate to supply the West. New Orleans was chosen as the perfect location for a new Branch Mint. It was at the head of the Mississippi, with all the access the river provided, and it was the key center for trade and commerce for the entire region.

In 1838, the New Orleans Mint started operations, and they began with the production of dimes and half dimes (Yes! Back then they had half dimes made of silver, instead of nickels). The value of Dimes and Half Dimes was too small to make a significant impact on the currency supply, so there was great pressure to begin production of half dollars. The half dollar was the largest silver coin being minted since 1803, and the production of large numbers of silver dollars wouldn't begin until 1840.

Mint Director, Robert Patterson, had two pairs of half dollar dies shipped to New Orleans in April 1838. These dies arrived in May and were put in storage in New Orleans, because the New Orleans Branch Mint had their hands full with problems producing dimes and half dimes on their small coin press. Also, the Half dollar coin press needed major fixing to make it operational, so no half dollars could be produced anyway. This delay didn't sit well with Mint Director Patterson, so on January 17, 1839, he wrote the following letter to New Orleans Branch Mint Superintendent David Bradford.

"It appears to me that no time should be lost in getting ready for the coinage of half dollars. Dimes and half dimes count too slowly, and keep your amount of coinage too low."

This was a clear directive to begin the production of half dollars FOR CIRCULATION as quickly as possible. The Mint Director's order was clear, but since the half dollar coin press wasn't operational yet, the Chief Coiner, Rufus Tyler, decided to try and make half dollars on the large dollar coin press instead. The problem with that plan was that the half dollar dies were too short to fit properly into the larger press. Tyler's half dollar run failed after exactly 10 coins were produced. On February 25, 1839, Tyler wrote the following letter to Mint Director Patterson.

"I mentioned in both of my former letters that the half dollar dies sent us last year are unsuitable for present use for besides being out of date the bottom ones are too short to reach the screws and consequently cannot be secured in the seats. I have however spliced one of them in order to try the press and succeeded in making ten excellent impressions, the very first one struck being as perfect as the dies, and entirely satisfactory, but the piece upon the bottom of the die became loose and I was unable to strike any more without fixing."

If the reverse die had not collapsed, Tyler would have been able to make thousands of 1838-O half dollars, and they wouldn't be rare today.

Patterson wrote back to Superintendent Bradford on March 15, 1839 that no more 1838-O half dollars be minted.

"I advise that the dies of 1838 be not used by you, that we have sometimes used the dies of a particular year for a few days after its close."

It isn't known if Tyler was able to fix the large dollar press for another run of half dollars AFTER his failure and BEFORE receiving Patterson's directive to stop. There aren't any letters in the National Archives one way or the other on this.

We do know that Tyler finally got the half dollar press running on March 27, 1839. Superintendent Bradford wrote the following to Patterson on March 29.

"I stated to Mr. Tyler that you advised that the dies of 1838 be not used and I suggested that it would be best to return them to you, thinking that they might serve some purpose, but he thought it not worthwhile. I have to request that you give me such direction in relation to the dies of 1838 now on hand in this Branch Mint as the case requires.

I have the pleasure of informing you that Mr. Tyler has got the half dollar coining press in operation. He commenced striking on the evening of the 27th inst ("inst" means "in this month") and the press is now performing admirably."

These four letters were discovered in the National Archives in the last twenty years. Before then, there was absolutely no mention of any production of these half dollars in any official Mint records.

We also know that Superintendent Bradford wanted to fire Rufus

Tyler, and he wrote to the Secretary of The Treasury (Levi Woodbury) to try to make it happen. There was a formal investigation with sworn depositions taken, and as a result of this investigation, Superintendent Bradford was fired and Tyler was retained.

Rufus Tyler died shortly after on September 8, 1839, during the annual Yellow Fever epidemic.

By the late 1880s, it was believed that as few as three 1838-O half dollars existed, and they were considered to be among the rarest of all American coins.

In 1893, Augustus Heaton published a book that detailed the scarcity of Branch mint coins for the very first time. He is generally credited with being "the father" of Mint Mark collecting. In his book, "A Treatise on the coinage of the Branch Mints of the United States," he prominently references the 1838-O half dollar as being one of the greatest of all mint mark rarities.

One year later, in 1894, an 1838-O half dollar was featured in a New York City auction, and it was purchased by Augustus Heaton himself. The coin had a note wrapped around it from Rufus Tyler to Alexander Dallas Bache, President of Girard College. That note was the VERY FIRST CLUE as to the origins of the 1838-O half dollar. Upon discovery of the note, it was immediately published by Ed. Frossard in the July 1894 edition of "The Numismatist," the leading coin journal of the day. Frossard's commentary, along with the text of that note, is as follows:

The comparative rarity of this half dollar has often formed a subject of discussion among collectors, some con-tending that only three specimens were struck, while others conceded a coinage of from twelve to fifteen pieces. In the recent Friesner sale, 583, the famed 1838 Orleans Mint half dollar , with O under the bust of Liberty on the obverse , was wrapped up in an old piece of paper on which was written the following statement which I have the pleasure to com-municate to The Numismatist for the benefit of its readers:

"The enclosed specimen coin of the United States Branch mint at New Orleans is presented to Pres. Bache by Rufus Tyler, the Coiner. It may be proper to state that not more than twenty pieces were struck with the half dollar dies of 1838."

This certificate in the handwriting of Rufus Tyler, should forever settle the question concerning the number of half dollars of the year 1838 issued at the New Orleans Mint. True "not more than twenty" is slightly vague - still it certainly means that the number was either twenty or a few less, say from fifteen to twenty and by these figures numismatist will hereafter have to abide.

The half dollar in question was purchased by Mr. A. G. Heaton, author of "Mint Marks" and of the "Twelve Silver Barons" and other very original and worthy compositions in verse which lately appeared in The Numismatist and the certificate has been presented to him by me through B. H. Collins, Esq.

While recent archival research has uncovered letters that detail the disastrous first run that failed after just 10 coins, there is absolutely no evidence as to if, where, when or how the additional coins were minted. David Stone and Mark VanWinkle have put forward the theory that there was a first test run in Philadelphia, and that most survivors are from that run because they don't show any die rust. They would have been placed in the Mint safe, accounting for their high survival rate in almost perfect condition. They also note that all these coins are PROOF, and Philadelphia was the only Mint at that time that made proofs. Their theory is strongly opposed by many experts who believe that ALL the half dollars were struck in New Orleans.

Now we have to add to this mix, the very strange Anderson DuPont specimen, which doesn't seem to fit anywhere and has NEVER been closely studied by anyone...expert or otherwise.

11

"Fish or Cut Bait"

I KNOW YOU'RE thinking, "WHAT KIND OF TREASURE HUNT IS THIS, if you have to spend $325, 000 JUST to get started?"

The Lagina brothers have invested MILLIONS in their Oak Island search, and Barry Clifford Invested MILLIONS looking for the Whydah wreck, so it can take some real money to get started. But, here's the thing. That money really isn't to get started. It's to LOCK UP your place! It's a bit like buying the right to drill for oil on a piece of land. It costs, but no one else can drill on that land, or hunt on Oak Island or search the wreck area claimed by Barry. YOU'VE bought that right! This is why it's so important to feel very, very sure that the treasure is where you think it is, BEFORE you pay out that kind of money. That means RESEARCH, RESEARCH and more RESEARCH! If the Lagina brothers are WRONG, and there's NO TREASURE LEFT on Oak Island, then they stand to lose everything they've invested. But EVEN THEN, there are ways to hedge that risk. With the Lagina brothers, the TV show on The History Channel is probably worth MORE than any treasure they'll ever find, and THAT'S a sure thing! You see what I mean? It's a lot of money, but even if they LOSE, they WIN! Before I lay out that kind of money, I have to feel sure I'm right, AND I have to find a way to hedge my bet, so if I'm wrong, at least I'll break even. With all that said, there's no reason in the world not to go after smaller treasure targets, where the upfront entry cost is less than $1,000, or even just $100! This is entirely up to your personal comfort and budget levels, but in every case it's still important to hedge your bet. That way, you won't lose, if things don't turn out as you hope. HEDGING is a FUNDAMENTAL RULE in internet treasure hunting!

So, now YOU know everything I know. I can get the money together to buy this thing, BUT it's a real stretch. The money is sitting in a money market account earning 0.0% interest because nothing earns any interest right now. I've talked with Patti about it many times over the past week, and she's ok either way. Would YOU do it?

This is like The Oak Island war room meeting.

"DON'T dig in the swamp!"

"YES! You HAVE to dig in the swamp!"

I'm really 50/50 on this venture. On the down side, it's a HUGE amount of money, and PROVING anything is going to be a great challenge. Stone and VanWinkle COULD have the answer, but NOTHING has been proven! Experts have been at this mystery for well more than 100 years, and they haven't solved it yet. And, by the way, I'm no expert! These guys have been in this business all their lives.

On the up side, really rare and possibly UNIQUE coins are worth millions, especially if they have provenance and a great story! This coin COULD have a history going all the way back to its striking in 1839, and it COULD have a great story IF it's the Alexander Dallas Bache coin that was auctioned in 1894.

Could I prove THAT? DIFFICULT, because truly PROVING anything is always hard, but NOT AT ALL IMPOSSIBLE, and HERITAGE already believes that part is true! The Anderson DuPont half dollar may not be the only one struck in New Orleans, BUT if I can PROVE it's the Tyler/Bache coin, then THAT alone will increase its value enough to hedge my bet. To PROVE that story, I'll have to become the WORLD'S EXPERT on the Anderson DuPont Specimen, and THAT will be relatively easy to do! While it's virtually impossible for me to become the leading expert on all rare American coins, it is less impossible for me to become the leading expert on half dollars dated 1838, and it's completely possible for me to become the world's leading expert on the Anderson DuPont 1838-O half dollar, because the area of focus is so narrow. This thought suddenly leads me to a totally weird vision.

I'm in a huge auditorium packed with several thousand people. There are no empty seats. I'm on the stage in front of this vast audience, and I'm about to be introduced by the man standing next to me. Behind us both is a giant floor to ceiling audio visual screen. Everyone is dressed in dark suits and white shirts. This is clearly a BIG DEAL occasion!

"Now I would like to introduce our KEYNOTE speaker. He is universally recognized as the word's leading expert on a penny he happened to get in change last week. Mr. CARMODY!" He gestures toward me and then exits the stage. Polite applause ripples through the audience as the screen behind me lights up. It shows the outside of a convenience store which then "morphs" into the inside, and shows a cashier at the counter.

"Here is where I made my purchase..." The slide changes again to show the picture of a tube of toothpaste.

"...of a tube of toothpaste."

There is a much louder round of applause.

"and HERE is the cashier, giving me a penny back in change from the $3 purchase price!"

The slide changes again, this time to show the cashier handing me a penny. The image grows, focusing in on just the penny until it fills the entire screen.

The applause is much, much louder now! I pause for it to die down, and then continue.

"This penny stayed in my pocket for two hours until I placed it on top of my bureau at home."

A close up picture of the penny on my bureau follows.

"AND, it remained there until this morning! AND..." I reach into my pocket and pull out the penny.

"HERE IT IS!"

The entire audience rises to their feet in a standing ova-
tion. They are overwhelmed by my depth of knowledge on
this subject. Later, someone is overheard saying "it's abso-
lutely AMAZING! No one in the entire world knows as much
about that penny as he does!"

My vision fades, and I'm left with the fleeting impression
that being the world's expert on just ONE coin is completely
possible, but a little bit absurd.

Tomorrow's the day I HAVE to call Ed and let him know one way or
the other about buying the coin. I can't put it off any longer.

It's Monday night, but Morris and Laura are out of town, so Patti
and I go to The Oakridge Pub by ourselves. After she finishes her THIRD
glass of Chardonnay, I bring up the subject of the coin and the decision
that needs to be made tomorrow.

"I've been doing a lot of research on this and even talked to Morris
about it, and I think it may be a pretty good investment even if it
NEVER turns into a home run. I think I CAN prove that this is the same
coin that was in the 1894 auction by showing that none of the others
COULD be that same 1894 coin. If I can do THAT, then I'd have established its history all the way back, AND I might even be able to change
its name! Those two things would make it a pretty good investment,
even if nothing else happens."

Patti looks at me very closely and says. "This ISN'T a llama farm,
is it?" We BOTH know exactly what that means. It's our code for an
investment that looks good, but ends up sucking you into something
you can't get out of.

About twenty years ago Patti and I went with a large
group of friends to stay at a "bed and breakfast" in upstate
New York. The B&B was owned by other friends, and it wasn't
doing very well (at all!). The idea was to help them out with
a big group spending the weekend AND lots of $. The couple

who owned the B&B also raised llamas. They thought the llamas would be fun for the guests, and they could breed them
to sell. They were all very tame and were even allowed inside
the house, BUT each one had to be wrapped in a disposable
diaper for obvious reasons. With the diaper securely in place,
the llamas could come and go anywhere they wanted. This
included bedrooms, bathrooms (for a quick refreshment!)
and the main living room. We'd be sitting there, and a couple
of llamas would wander in just like other guests. It also included the kitchen, which turned out to be a very bad idea.
You may not know this about llamas. They'll try to eat almost
anything. If they see it, they'll try to eat it! Also, they can be
somewhat fussy about what they've already put in their om-
nivorous mouths. If they don't happen to like their particular
choice of the moment, they'll just spit it out...on the floor,
on the rug, on any convenient chair and on any guest who
happened to be closest. This resulted in the rather unfortunate practice by our hosts of cutting off parts of the food that
had been "sampled" (especially sandwiches, bread, cheese,
fruit and every possible kind of dessert), in order to salvage
the untouched parts for their paying guests. Fortunately, the
llamas didn't care too much for meat, so that gave me at
least one food safe haven. "Safe" is a relative term. While
the meat never actually entered their mouths, they sniffed it
to the point where it looked like they were going suck it up
their noses. When they decided they didn't like the smell, the
process was reversed, ending with a giant "SNORT," which
pretty much obliterated the meat tray. Obviously, you can't
diaper both ends of a llama, so we had to live with this little
inconvenience.

The other half of this "llama lunacy" was breeding them
to sell. How did THAT go, you may ask? NOT well! NOT well
at all! There are two problems with breeding llamas for sale.
The first problem is entirely predictable. In short order, you'll

have lots of llamas running around. The cost of disposable diapers alone would lead to bankruptcy. As a result, there wouldn't be any more room for paying guests since llamas would occupy every room in the house. Also, you can forget food. It's ALL gone, even the meat!

The second problem is one our hosts didn't see until well after they got into this business. The ONLY people who want to BUY llamas are people who want to start another llama farm to sell llamas to other would be llama farmers. The whole thing is a giant Ponzi scheme, and our friends discovered they couldn't even give them away, let alone SELL them.

One final thought. Petting a llama is like petting a wool rug!

I reassure Patti that the 1838-O isn't another llama farm, and she tells me whatever I want to do will be OK! Tomorrow, I'll have to decide whether to "fish" or "cut bait!"

12

Schrödinger Pays a Visit

THAT NIGHT, I have a fitful and restless sleep filled with anxiety riddled dreams, all driven by the decision I have to make the next day. I awake at 6am with one of those dreams still lingering in my mind. I was at a card table, and the top was covered with jig saw puzzle pieces. Some were right side up and some were upside down, but none had been connected to any other. There was no box to tell what the picture was, and I was feeling extremely anxious, like I was running out of time to finish a final exam. The pieces not only didn't fit, but they didn't make sense either! It was as if there were pieces from a bunch of different puzzles all mixed up together. Underneath my overwhelming feeling of anxiety, there was a persistent scratching sound that seemed to get louder. It was coming from outside my back door, so I got up from the table, went to the door and opened it. There was a large orange cat with a silver chain and tag around its neck. The cat seemed very friendly, as he looked up and "meowed" at me. I bent down, picked him up and gently cradled him in my arms. The cat "meowed" again and tilted his head so I could rub him behind the ears and under his chin. He started purring. The silver tag said "Schrödinger," and the card table, with all its puzzle pieces, had disappeared.

I wake up.

I'm not really surprised at this dream. I've been in a state of anxiety ever since Ed called ten days ago, and the whole story about the 1838-O half dollar is a maddening puzzle.

In thinking about Schrödinger, I didn't know he was orange, and I don't know why he was in my dream.

Now that I think about it, this half dollar is just like my Buttersworth painting. It may be just like all the other half dollars, only in poorer condition, or it may be something unique and very special. Right now, it's BOTH, it has the potential to be either, as soon as Schrödinger's box is opened. In this case, the box is the 1838-O mystery. Solve the mystery, and the box is opened! There is one other thing too. I'm the only one who thinks my Buttersworth might be real, but two of the experts at the world's largest numismatic auction house believe the Anderson DuPont half dollar is "real."

I started doing hard jig saw puzzles with my daughter Lindsey when she was about nine. The very first one we ever did was a jungle scene, with all kinds of wild animals hidden among the dense jungle vines and leaves. We had the top of the box, so we knew what the picture looked like, and that helped us figure out where the harder pieces were supposed to go. As Lindsey got older we finally agreed that looking at the picture was cheating. At the very center was the black head of a panther, with golden yellow eyes staring right at us. First, we found the four corners, and then we checked every single piece to separate out all the edge pieces. It took two days, but we finally completed the border, and then we started to fill in the middle. We'd each take an animal and try to complete it. Lindsey took the elephant and found all the grey pieces, while I worked on the lions with their tawny orange pieces. Once we'd mostly completed an animal, we'd check the box cover and then place our animal inside the puzzle border where they seemed to belong. After four more days, we were nearly done, and we were linking the animals to the borders and to each other. At last, we were filling in the jungle leaves between the animals, and each remaining piece seemed to find its proper place faster and faster. BUT, the head of the panther, with its golden eyes, was still missing. Finally, Lindsey put her last piece into place, but the head was STILL missing. At that point, I said to her "OHHHH... WAIT!"

I slowly reached into my pocket, making sure she was closely watching my every move, and I pulled out the one last piece.

"Why, what on earth could THIS possibly be?" I said, and then I very slowly placed the panther head into the last open spot in the puzzle.

Her eyes got larger and larger. She looked at me, and her little eyes started to narrow into a squint.

"THAT'S NOT FAIR," she squealed.

She ripped the panther head out of the center of the puzzle, held it up and wiggled it right in front of my eyes. Then she gently placed the panther head back into its empty space, while making sure I was watching HER. Once it was in place, she gently patted it, and looked back up at me.

"NOW it's done," she exclaimed!

My harmless little life's lesson had some unintended consequences. From that point on, whenever we'd do a puzzle together DOZENS of pieces were always missing. We both had our pockets stuffed with potential last pieces. The end always turned into a piece by piece negotiation, a bit like an arms control treaty, with each side giving up missiles one at a time.

The Panther head was the very last time I ever got to put in the last puzzle piece with my daughter.

The 1838-O half dollar is the last great unsolved Numismatic mystery of the nineteenth century, and it would be a great adventure to try and solve it. You might ask how I could possibly solve something that none of the experts have been able to do over the past 120 years, when I don't know much of anything about coins. I really don't think I can, but I COULD have one advantage over everyone else. IF I buy the Anderson DuPont half dollar, I might very well have the "panther head" in my pocket, and it COULD be the key to the entire mystery. I DO believe I can PROVE that it's the same coin that had the famous Tyler letter wrapped around it, and that would give it a "provenance" going all the way back to The Chief Coiner of the New Orleans Mint in 1839. THAT would make the Anderson DuPont specimen the most historically important 1838-O half dollar. THAT would be my "hedge" to make sure I wouldn't lose anything, IF I make this bet.

At 11am I call Ed and tell him I've decided to buy the coin.

13

Brinksmanship

NO! NOT THAT kind of "brinksmanship." The OTHER kind, as in "BRINKS" armored car.

The phone rings!

"Hello?"

"This is Stevens Armored Car service. Is this Mr. Carmody?"

"Yes?"

I answer in a question, even though I know my own name. I wasn't expecting an armored car to come calling.

"We have a delivery for you. Will you be home in an hour?"

"Yes...maybe..."

"Good, we'll be at your house in one hour. You'll need to show us some identification, before we can turn over the package."

"Identification?"

"Yes. Birth certificate, passport, driver's license, and some bills with your name and your current address on them. Nothing complicated. No DNA tests, or sworn and notarized affidavits from neighbors, or anything like THAT!"

"Good to hear it's not complicated. I like that!"

"See you in an hour."

I thought the Anderson DuPont coin was going to arrive in a U.S. mail truck, but apparently it's being delivered by a SWAT team of uniformed guards, carrying machine guns and driving a steel plated tank. WHAT have I gotten myself into, and WHAT will the neighbors think? First things first! The neighbors can wait. I HAVE a driver's license, but it'll take a little searching to come up with the rest of the "uncomplicated" items. I don't want to face these people without all the right "proof" in my hands! Patti sees me rummaging through our papers and asks.

"What's going on?"

"I think the coin is about to be delivered."

"Maybe it's something else," she says.

I think about that for a bit.

"No! I'm pretty sure it's the coin." I counter, without mentioning the armored car.

It was supposed to arrive about noon. A huge armored car, that looked like it was straight out of a movie, was going to park right in front of our house. All the neighbors would be peering out their windows OR, more likely, running out into the street to see what was going on. At the very moment they were all gathered outside my house, the doors of the car/tank would open and a SWAT team would rush the front door. I can see it plain as day. The leader signals a forward motion with his raised right arm, two guards take covering positions, while two more flank either side of my front door. Another forward hand gesture brings four more guards from out of the car/tank carrying a tiny box. There are two on each side, so they have it fully protected from any possible assault, and they run with the box to my front door in crouched positions, no doubt to make smaller targets for any possible snipers in the gathering crowd.

This is NOT good!

I could even imagine potential criminals in the crowd talking to each other.

"You know, I never really thought about robbing THAT house, but maybe we should reconsider!"

The coin AND my Buttersworth would both be gone by morning, but on the bright side, maybe they'd take Patti's collection of antique

Chinese locks shaped like insects as long as they were there anyway.

It turns out I'm overly worried for nothing! The armored car looks more like a heavy duty SUV than like a Brinks truck, and there is only the driver...no SWAT team. While the driver DOES have a pistol, he isn't even in uniform, so there was nothing exciting to rile up the crowd, which never gathered in the first place.

I hand my ID papers to the driver, and he looks them over quickly, and then has me sign for the package. Once that's done, he goes back to his car and brings out a small package. It's VERY small, given all the fuss and bother. I open it in front of him, just to make sure the box isn't empty, and this whole thing isn't a scam. I know it isn't, but it would truly be awful if I opened it up after he had left, and then discovered there was nothing inside. Once the wrapping is off, I see a small rectangular walnut wooden case. The top is on brass hinges and snaps open when I lift it. There's a black inset liner with a space perfectly cut to fit the coin in it's holder, and the Anderson DuPont 1838-O half dollar is securely set in that space. I click the box shut, tell the driver everything's fine, and he leaves without the slightest stir from any of my neighbors.

Once inside, I open the box and show it to Patti, but this would be a very quick visitation. I want to get it into my safe deposit box as quickly as possible before the thieves get wind of this deal. I look at the coin more closely. It has a dark sooty appearance, which actually looks somewhat elegant in its white holder set inside its polished walnut box. At that moment, the coin's REAL name comes to me. I'll call it THE CINDERELLA COIN. The name fits perfectly, because its true nature has been hidden for all these years. Like Cinderella, it has ashes on its face, and it's little more than a poor soot covered orphan when compared to her eight beautiful sisters. Its lineage only goes back to the 1954 Anderson DuPont sale, but it's really a long lost princess just waiting to be discovered! I absolutely hate the "Anderson DuPont" name, and I swore to change it if I ever bought the coin. From now on, it will be THE CINDERELLA COIN, but it'll take a lot more than just me, for the rest of the world to accept THAT new name. I'll have to PROVE that this coin really is a "princess" in disguise, if THE CINDERELLA COIN name is to have any chance of sticking. I'll also have to have a different name that reflects its history on its holder.

IF I can PROVE the linkage to the 1894 auction and the Tyler letter, I'll have the name TYLER/BACHE put on the holder, and ANDERSON DUPONT will be gone forever!

With those thoughts fresh in my mind, I run upstairs with the coin and box in hand. I grab my safe deposit key, rush downstairs and out to my car. Five minutes later, I'm in the bank, and five minutes after that, I'm home again.

The Cinderella coin is locked up in her new safe deposit box prison, and for the first time since Ed called two weeks ago, my heart rate finally drops to something approaching normal.

14

Another Monday with Morris

THAT FOLLOWING MONDAY finds us once again at the Oakridge Pub for dinner with Morris and Laura. It's been a long time since our last get together. He doesn't know I've bought the coin, and IT will be my treasure hunt target!

Morris and Laura arrive, but Morris has a noticeable limp.

"Hi Morris!...What happened to you? You're limping!"

Morris had hurt his back lifting some boxes, and that had ruined his golf swing, along with his entire golf game. When he tried to adjust his swing, he hurt his ankle. His hurt ankle forced him to change his swing again, which re injured his back. Things had gone from bad to worse in a very short time.

"I'm thinking of giving it up!" he says. At The Landings, there's never any need to say what "IT" is that's being given up, because "IT" is ALWAYS golf. People don't smoke as much as they used to, and there's no smoking in the clubs, so smoking is never "IT" anymore. Anyway, when talking about smoking, they always say "I'm thinking about QUITTING." You can't "QUIT" golf, because then you'd be a "Quitter." Being a "Quitter" would brand you for life, but you can THINK about giving it up. THINKING about giving IT up, and actually giving IT up are two totally different things. The only people I ever knew who actually gave IT up, are people who died, usually on the golf course. The reason for this brief digression, is that I'm trying to understand and speak fluent " golf," so I can better communicate with the native population, and respect their local customs and rituals.

"I'm doing some back exercises that should help." Morris says, clearly indicating that he'd be back on the golf course, as soon as he could walk. Golfers ARE persistent, I'll say that for them!

Finally, Morris asks; "How's your treasure hunt going?"

THIS was my opening, and I couldn't wait to tell him!

"GREAT!...so far. I bought a very rare coin!"

"You BOUGHT your treasure! Doesn't that sort of defeat the whole purpose of treasure hunting?"

"NO!...well maybe...sort of...ummm...if you put it THAT way! You HAVE to look at it like Oak Island. The treasure isn't just sitting there waiting to be scooped up. The Lagina brothers have to INVEST lots of money in heavy drilling equipment to go after their treasure. It's the SAME thing here."

Actually, I recall that in the heat of the moment, I DID tell Morris that there was treasure everywhere, and that you could practically trip over it, but I'm hoping he's forgotten that little bit of exaggeration.

Not unexpectedly, he asks "How much?"

"Quite expensive, but it's worth it...and It has a GREAT story!"

I'm not about to tell him how much it cost, so I quickly open my laptop to show him a picture.

Morris looks at the picture, and his right eyebrow rises in an expression of surprise. The image of Morris as Marty Lagina evaporates, and is instantly replaced with Morris as "Mr. Spock" from StarTrek, except his ears aren't pointy enough. Just like the antique dealer who captured the essence of my Buttersworth in just one word, he was able to do the same with my new coin.

"It's BLACK!" he says.

"Yes! Yes it is! That's part of its mystery and charm! THAT'S why I've decided to call it the 'Cinderella' coin."

Morris doesn't press the issue.

"So, what do you do now?" He asks.

"NOW, I have to research MY coin as much as possible to establish its PROVENANCE!"

I place maximum emphasis on "MY" and "PROVENANCE," but Morris seems unimpressed, and his face remains totally blank. He must not watch the Antiques Roadshow.

I'm afraid his Spock-inner self will say "ILLOGICAL," so I retreat to much safer ground.

"SO! You're REALLY going to give IT up?"

15

The 1838 -O Puzzle

HUNTING FOR TREASURE at home is a little like digging for treasure on Oak Island.

In both cases, we're looking for clues that will solve the mystery and lead to the treasure. On Oak Island, they have to dig real holes in real dirt to find their clues. In our case, we're going to have to dig virtual holes in the online information base to find our clues. This includes The National Archives, Ancestry websites and online Numismatic information, such as images and previous research. This process is like Oak Island in that one clue will give us some idea where we should "dig" for more clues, and where we should STOP digging.

The BEST metaphor is still the jigsaw puzzle. At this point, the border of the puzzle isn't complete yet. No one knows the boundaries that define the production of the 1838-O half dollars. Did production start with proofs made in 1838 in Philadelphia, as Dave Stone and I believe, OR did production began with PROOFS in January 1839 in New Orleans, as most other experts believe? Was there more than one production run in New Orleans, and if so, when did production finally end? Once the border is finished, and by "finished" I mean PROVEN, then it will be possible to insert each of the nine known specimens into their proper place, just like the animals in my jungle puzzle. Only then will we be able to see the whole picture and understand WHY everything happened as it did, and WHY this has been such a great unsolved mystery for more than 150 years. The main problem is that when Lindsey and I did the Jungle puzzle, we had ALL the pieces on our table right in front of us. In this case, we have some pieces, but we'll need a lot more to have any chance of solving this thing.

Here are all the puzzle pieces we have so far.

9 pieces representing each of the 9 surviving coins.

1 piece for the Philadelphia Mint.

1 piece for the New Orleans Mint.

6 pieces for the 6 main characters:

-Secretary of the Treasury LEVI WOODBURY

-Mint Director ROBERT PATTERSON

-New Orleans Branch Mint Superintendent DAVID BRADFORD

-Chief Coiner NewOrleans Branch Mint RUFUS TYLER

-ALEXANDER DALLAS BACHE, who received the 1838-O half dollar from Tyler

-AUGUSTUS HEATON, who purchased the coin in 1894

1 piece for the 1954 Anderson DuPont auction.

1 piece for the January 15, 1839 letter from Mint Director Patterson to Bradford directing him to start production of half dollars for circulation.

1 piece for the February 25, 1839 letter from Tyler to Patterson telling him that he had made exactly 10 coins before the production run failed, and no more could be made "without further fixing."

1 piece for the March 15, 1839 letter from Patterson to Bradford ordering him to cease any further production of 1838-O half dollars.

1 piece for the March 29, 1839 letter from Bradford to Patterson stating that he had received and passed on the order to cease 1838 production, and that Tyler had started production of 1839-O half dollars on the evening of March 27.

1 piece for the presentation note that Tyler wrote to Bache that was found wrapped around the specimen auctioned in 1894. This note stated that "not more than twenty" were made.

1 piece for the June 13, 1839 letter from Bradford to Patterson

stating that the front (obverse) dies had been destroyed.

It's important to mention that the letters referenced above were mostly uncovered by noted Numismatic Researcher R. W. Julian in numerous exhaustive searches of the National Archives in Philadelphia that hold all the records for the U.S. Mint. It's extremely unlikely that he missed anything in his searches, so it's unlikely that any more important letters will ever turn up from this source.

We have 24 pieces of the puzzle so far, and SOME of those pieces can be connected. The "end border" is defined, because no production of 1838-O half dollars could possibly have occurred after June 13, 1839, when the dies were destroyed. In addition, the first New Orleans production run is well defined by the first 3 archival letters. We KNOW that exactly 10 coins were produced FOR CIRCULATION during this run, and that Tyler had to splice the reverse die in place, because it was too short for the large dollar press. It was the collapse of this support system for the reverse die that ended the run after only 10 coins.

With these pieces in hand, the next question is WHERE DO WE START DRILLING TO FIND MORE PIECES?

Where would YOU start?

For me, that decision is easy! I want to PROVE that the coin I bought (the Anderson DuPont specimen) is the same one that had the note wrapped around it and was auctioned in 1894.

IF I can PROVE that, then I can change its name and establish its lineage all the way back to Chief Coiner Rufus Tyler.

That alone would justify its purchase, THAT is my HEDGE, and THAT'S where we'll start!

16

The Road to Provenance

THERE ARE EIGHT other 1838-O half dollars, and I have to prove that none of the other eight COULD have been in the 1894 auction. IF I can do THAT, then my coin must be the one that had the note wrapped around it and was in the 1894 auction.

We KNOW the History of the Tyler/Bache coin up to a point. It was purchased in June 1894 by Augustus Heaton and remained in his collection until his death in 1930.

Heaton's collection was sold intact to Waldo Newcomer, and Newcomer's collection was sold intact to Col.E.H. Green in 1933. There isn't any record after that, so there's a timeline gap that needs to be filled in to link it to the Anderson DuPont sale in 1954.

Because the Tyler/Bache coin remained in the collections of Heaton, Newcomer and Green from 1894 through 1935, any specimen that had ANY auction or Convention appearance during that 40 year period COULD NOT have been the CINDERELLA COIN.

HERE's the history of the other eight coins.

THE SMITHSONIAN SPECIMEN

This one is automatically eliminated, because it's been in the Mint collection since 1839.

THE ELIASBERG SPECIMEN

This one is eliminated because it was auctioned in Jan 1890. The 1894 "Numismatist" article indicates the Tyler/Bache coin was a RECENTLY discovered specimen "with a note wrapped around it." Obviously, it couldn't be recently discovered AND the same one auctioned just four years earlier.

THE NORWEB SPECIMEN

This one is eliminated because it was auctioned by E. Frossard in October 1884 and again in October 1908. Tyler/Bache specimen was still in Heaton's collection in 1908.

THE ATWATER SPECIMEN

This one is eliminated because Numismatic historical records show that Atwater "discontinued collecting in the 1920's." The Tyler/Bache specimen was still in Heaton's collection at that time.

THE BALDENHOFER SPECIMEN

There is no history of this specimen prior to the "Green" collection, so it can't be eliminated on the basis of auction appearances. However, this specimen IS graded as PROOF 64, and this is way too high to be the 1894 auction coin. What's more, this one is a "brilliant" proof, which means it has mirror-like surfaces, and the 1894 auction coin has no mirrored surfaces at all. Its surfaces are referred to as "opaque" or dark, rather than "shiny."

THE COX SPECIMEN

There is no history of this specimen prior to the "Green" collection, so it can't be eliminated on the basis of auction appearances. However, like the BALDENHOFFER specimen, it's also a "brilliant proof" with highly mirrored and reflective surfaces, and this is inconsistent with the 1894 auction coin.

THE NEIL SPECIMEN

This one is eliminated, because it was displayed at the 1914 ANS convention by H.O. Granberg. The Tyler/Bache specimen was still in Heaton's collection in 1914.

THE BOYD- GUGGENHEIMER SPECIMEN

This one is eliminated because it was in the Chapman auction of October 1888 and sold to Virgil Brand in February 1902. The Tyler/ Bache specimen was still in Heaton's collection in 1902.

Through a combination of prior auction, convention display appearances and surface characteristics, we can conclude that Anderson DuPont is the ONLY specimen that could possibly be the Tyler/Bache specimen. The next step is to contact The Numismatic Guarantee Company (NGC) to see if they'll accept my evidence. NGC is one of the most respected Numismatic certification companies in the world, so if they agree, then everyone will agree. The way I'll do this is by asking if they'll change the holder label to read "EX TYLER /BACHE," which is the provenance of the 1894 auction coin, based on the note wrapped around it from Rufus Tyler to Alexander Dallas Bache.

A week later I get the response back from NGC, and NOW I understand why Heritage says ANDERSON DUPONT is MOST LIKELY the same coin. They're extremely supportive of my effort, BUT I haven't got solid PROOF that they are one and the same. The problem is that at least four of the 1838-O half dollars ended up in the collection of Col. E.H. Green, so there's no proof that just because it went into that collection, it's the same one that came out the other side and ended up in the Anderson DuPont auction. It's POSSIBLE that the Tyler/Bache coin was destroyed or lost sometime during the period 1935 and 1954, and the Anderson DuPont specimen is an entirely different coin that was discovered at a later date and then bought by Anderson DuPont. After all, the Tyler note indicates that 20 were made and only 9 are accounted for. It COULD be one of those other missing 11 coins. In order to satisfy NGC, I have to PROVE that the Anderson DuPont specimen was actually purchased from the Green collection.

Several years ago, Patti, Lindsey and I went on a safari to Tanzania. We walked over a suspension bridge that spanned the Gremetti River with dozens of crocodiles below, all desperately hoping for the slightest misstep. It didn't help much when Lindsey and I started bouncing on the bridge to see if we could get their attention. We already had their attention, BUT it did cause them to open their mouths as wide as possible.

We went out to the Serengeti to see the great migration, which is mostly Wildebeest, Zebra, some Giraffe AND lots of lions following this mobile buffet. The Wildebeest and the Zebras were everywhere, but the Lions weren't so easy to spot. Lions are just very large cats, and as everyone knows, cats don't seem have any bones...at least none that are connected. So this means that when the Lions lie down (which they do 23 hours a day because THAT'S what cats do!), you can't see them, even in grass that's only a foot high. They're like cat rugs! Flat as a pancake! BUT, our guide taught us how to spot Lions. The reason the Wildebeest and Zebras like to migrate together is because Wildebeest are as blind as bats, but can smell a blade of tasty grass a mile a way. The Zebras can't SMELL a Lion if they're standing right on top of one, BUT they can SEE a delicious succulent herb two miles away. So if you want to find a bunch of Lions out on the Serengeti, all you have to do is look for a bunch of Zebras standing in a line and staring intently at absolutely nothing. They're actually staring at a pile of flat Lion rugs that you can't see. Here's the point of this story. Our guide then told us the reason that

Zebras have stripes is natural camouflage. THAT seemed pretty amazing to me, because a Zebra is absolutely, without any doubt, the easiest thing to spot in all of Africa BECAUSE of its black and white stripes. Our guide was RIGHT, and it has to do with the way Lions hunt. The pride of Lions pick out one specific Zebra for lunch, and then try to go after it . Once all the Zebras get into a panic mode because of the Lions and start running every which way, it makes it easy for the main course to get lost in the total confusion of black and white stripes. I guess THIS is why there aren't any all black Zebras. They were all eaten a long time ago!

This is the same problem that NGC has with the CINDERELLA COIN. It's possible to track it as long as it's standing all by itself, but once it disappeared into Col. Greens "herd" of 1838-O's, there's no PROVING which one is which after that.

I'd need MORE proof, and THAT would have to come from the Anderson DuPont coin's distinctive color. If it's like a black Zebra, then maybe it can be tracked into the herd on one side and out again on the other.

17

Tracking an All Black Zebra

HOW CAN WE go about tracking our all black Zebra? The first thing to do is to get a copy of Ed. Frossard's July 1894 auction catalogue and look at the listing for the TYLER/BACHE (CINDERELLA) coin. I'm hoping that the American Numismatic Association has a copy in their library Archives, after all they're located in New York, and the 1894 auction took place in New York. Their librarian returns my call two days later, and says:

"NO, we don't have a COPY. We have Frossard's ORIGINAL brochure. May I make a copy for you?"

The copy arrives in a week, and it contains some VERY interesting new information. Augustus Heaton's initials are right next to the listing for the Tyler/Bache coin, but there's absolutely NO mention of any note in the brochure. If there had been a note at that time, it would have been a most important part of this listing. Its absence means that Heaton asked about the origins of this rare coin AFTER he bought it in JUNE 1894, and the note was then found and published in JULY 1894. The very fact that this note ("an old scrap of paper") could have been recovered before it was thrown away means that it was probably in an album, and the coin had been removed for sale just a few short years before the 1894 auction.

Most importantly, the actual listing says the coin is "UNCIRCULATED" and not PROOF, and that it is "OPAQUE." OPAQUE means that the coin has NO shiny reflective surfaces. This is critically important, because ANDERSON DUPONT is the ONLY KNOWN surviving specimen that doesn't have reflective mirror-like surfaces. THIS is a key link between the two coins.

The next question to answer is "Why is Anderson DuPont black?" The discoloration doesn't appear to be due to fire, because there aren't any scorch or burn marks. It seems to be most likely some kind of toning.

The next step is to figure out how that kind of toning or discoloration could occur. The most obvious place to look is the note that was wrapped around the coin. After all, the coin was inside that note for 50+ years, and it would've been tough for something else to get inside, especially if the note and coin were kept in an album.

I go on the internet to learn everything I can about early 19th century note paper, and the results of that search point to the next place to dig for clues. Early 19th century paper was made using sulfur based chemicals, and the paper itself would have had a very high sulfur content. Our digging target is the chemical interaction between sulfur and silver, as in the case of a silver half dollar. The answer comes back very quickly! Sulfur tarnishes silver. On silver coins, that tarnishing is called "toning," and it can result in absolutely spectacular colors. Old coins exposed to sulfur in the air can have a rainbow of reds, golds, blues, oranges, greens and all the colors in between. They are prized for their beauty and often command much higher prices than their "untoned" counterparts. However, too much or too long exposure to sulfur causes the toning to go all the way to BLACK! It's clear from all the information available on "toning" that ANY coin wrapped in a piece of 19th century paper for 50+ years would HAVE TO BE BLACK (or "opaque" if you want to use a somewhat gentler word). This is a major piece of evidence, because Anderson Dupont is the ONLY specimen that has that essential feature. All the others are the exact opposite of opaque, with bright, shiny mirror-like surfaces.

So, now we have an all black Zebra going INTO Col. Green's herd, and we have a black Zebra in the 1954 Anderson DuPont auction. Is it possible to track our black Zebra OUT of Col. Green's herd?

David Stone of Heritage gives me a lead. He suggests I contact Leonard Augsberger, who has the complete ledgers of Burdette Johnson's purchases from Col Green's collection. He's just one of a number of people who bought coins from Green's estate, but it's worth a shot. I write Leonard and ask if he has seen any records of the purchase of an 1838-O half dollar in his ledgers. He tells me that it may take a couple of weeks, but he'll see if he can check it out for me. There's no reason in the world for him to do this, other than his own generosity and his love of Numismatics.

In about three weeks I get a very apologetic letter from Leonard. He's found just ONE sales reference for an 1838-O half dollar in the Burdette Johnson ledger, but there's no picture, no description and no other written information that could link it to my coin. He's sorry he couldn't be of more help, but in closing he does mention a very odd notation above the listing . It's only one word in parentheses, and he has no idea what it means. The word is "BLACK."

The very next stop is another letter to NGC with all the new evidence, and one month later I have their response. All their experts have reviewed my evidence and they agree! If I resubmit the coin, they'll re label it "EX TYLER /BACHE."

The "ANDERSON DUPONT" specimen name will be gone forever! From now on, it will be known as the "TYLER/BACHE" specimen with one of the most interesting and colorful stories. It will have one of the longest unbroken histories in all of American Numismatics.

While TYLER/BACHE is its new Numismatic name, I'm hoping its common name will become "THE CINDERELLA COIN." It's not enough to establish the PROVENANCE all the way back to Rufus Tyler in 1839 for the "Cinderella" name to apply, we will need to prove she's something special as compared to all the other 1838-O half dollars. We have to PROVE that Tyler/Bache is a REAL PRINCESS!

We've FINALLY linked a couple of puzzle pieces. We've linked the Tyler/Bache 1894 auction coin to the Anderson DuPont specimen, and that links it to the failed first New Orleans production run in January 1839. No other 1838-O half dollar has any kind of proven linkage to a specific production date or location, but this is just a start. The hardest part is yet to come, and THAT will be to find all the missing pieces and then put them together to solve this mystery.

18

Alexander Dallas Bache and the Missing Note

The Tyler/Bache Coin and Anderson DuPont are one and the same, BUT there is still a 55 year gap between the time the coin was given to Alexander Dallas Bache in 1839 and the time it was auctioned in 1894. We want to fill in that gap as much as we can, and maybe even find the lost Tyler letter.

It's virtually certain that the Tyler/Bache Coin with the note wrapped around it remained in the Bache family for nearly all that time. Every coin collector of the day knew about the rarity and mystery of the 1838-O half dollar, so both the importance of the coin and the note would have been instantly recognized and publicized, if they'd been in anyone else's hands. IF they had gone into anyone else's hands, the coin and note would have been unwrapped and separated, if only to see what was inside. They were NOT unwrapped and remained together.

We also know that Bache never went to New Orleans and Tyler never went to Philadelphia during 1839, so the coin and note couldn't have been presented in person by Tyler. The coin with the note wrapped around it had to have been SENT by Tyler to Bache. That's how they were received, and that's how they remained for about 50 years. As Frossard wrote, the note was just an " old scrap of paper", so it would have been lost almost as soon as it was separated from the coin. We HAVE to conclude that the coin and note remained in the Bache family in a place where they'd stay together over several generations. That place couldn't have been a desk drawer or an old box. It HAD to be a family album ! If we can find the Bache family album, we'll almost certainly find the 50 year hiding place of the coin and note and perhaps even the envelop it came in, but this hunt won't be easy after 120 years.

When Lindsey was little, I'd hide Easter eggs for her, and she LOVED the hunt. The first time, she was just short of her second birthday, and I scattered little red, green, blue, gold and silver foil wrapped chocolate eggs all over our red shag carpet, so they'd be easy to find and gather. I gave her a little wicker basket filled with green plastic "hay" and off she went! You parents already know THIS was a big mistake, but I was a new parent and this was our first family Easter egg hunt, so there's a little bit of a learning curve. Naturally, she just dropped the basket on the spot, and started picking up the eggs and stuffing them into her mouth...still in their foil wrappers of course! I had to pry open her mouth to remove eggs as if I were her dentist extracting teeth, If she HAD any teeth, and thank goodness the ones she had were small and not too sharp! As soon I got one egg out, she had two more in her hands ready to go in. You'd think that would've turned her off to Easter eggs, but NO!

It's still her second favorite holiday next to Halloween, because she LOVES the hunt!

As she got older, I'd hide the eggs in harder and harder places, so the hunt became much more important than the eggs themselves. The last time, she was 15, and I put a basket full of chocolate eggs in a glass front Secretary in plain sight, where she'd spot it immediately. I locked the Secretary doors and then taped the key to the back of a picture hanging in a different room. *NO WAY would she ever find THAT! Within ten minutes, she walked into the living room carrying her Easter basket.*

"HOW on EARTH did you find the key so fast?"

"So VERY easy!" She said in a dismissive tone and with a self satisfied smirk on her face." You're just SLIPPING in your old age."

"I DON'T believe it!" I said, "You must have been spying on me when I hid the key!"

I ran into the other room with Lindsey right on my heels and turned over the picture.

Of course the key was still taped to the back. She hadn't even bothered to look for it! She just picked the lock instead.

The next year Lindsey came to me and said "Dad, I've hidden ONE egg in the kitchen, and I BET you can't find it!"

REVENGE is a terrible thing to witness, especially when it happens to you!

"I CAN'T find it??? Oh REALLY??"

The die was cast, the gauntlet thrown and the challenge accepted! I gathered wrenches, screwdrivers, hammers, pliers and every other tool known to man, even if I didn't have the slightest idea what it was for or how to use it. THEN, I got a roll of yellow "CRIME SCENE DO NOT CROSS" tape. I was READY!

I went through that kitchen inch by inch, taking apart cabinets, removing drawers, dismantling coffee machines and unscrewing floor drains. After each section had suffered through my "scorched earth" search, I'd move my Crime Scene tape and start on another section. I took apart the dishwasher and I painstakingly studied every piece of garbage in the trash bin.

I even probed the garbage disposal (while doing THAT, I taped the switch in the "off" position just to avoid any unfortunate accident). I completely emptied the refrigerator and checked every single item including liquid cartons of milk and orange juice, I even checked the eggs to make sure she hadn't pulled some shenanigans like carefully opening one up and then gluing it back together again.

NOTHING!

Finally in desperation, I checked all my clothes. After all, I was in the kitchen, so I counted too.

After 3 fruitless hours of battle, I waved the white flag and surrendered.

"WHERE ever did you hide it?" I asked in a totally defeated tone.

She smiled a very, very condescending smile and casually walked over to the refrigerator and opened the freezer drawer.

She reached in and took out a three pound package of frozen hamburger that was right on top and pointed to the middle.

"I bought this package of hamburger, carefully opened it, put the egg in the very middle, rewrapped it and then FROZE it."

I stood there in disbelief, and then she added

"I KNEW you'd NEVER thaw two hundred dollars worth of frozen groceries just to find ONE tiny Easter egg."

So, I've had wartime experience in hunting! In searching for long lost letters, documents or items, it can help to build a family tree. The things you're searching for may have been passed down to later generations, and you can find clues in Wills and other court documents. The first thing I do in hunting for the lost Bache family album (IF it even exists), is to create a BACHE family tree using Ancestry.com.

Alexander. Dallas Bache (1806 - 1867)
Image courtesy of NOAA

Alexander Dallas Bache was born in Philadelphia July 19, 1806.

He was the Great grandson of Benjamin Franklin and went to West Point where he roomed with Alexander Stevens, the future Vice President of the Confederacy. He later became a professor of Engineering at West Point and then Professor of "Natural Philosophy" (Physics) at the University of Pennsylvania. This is the same position that Robert Patterson held before becoming Director of the U.S. Mint, and the two became lifelong friends.

Bache became President of Girard College in Philadelphia in 1838, and embarked on a year long study tour of European educational institutions as background for his new position.

This is the title he held when Tyler wrote his presentation note that was wrapped around the coin. Tyler died shortly thereafter of yellow fever on Sept. 8, 1839 in New Orleans. Tyler's obituary was published in THE SPRINGFIELD REPUBLICAN on September 28, 1839, and it can be inferred from the text that he left no family.

> *At New Orleans, on the 8th inst. of the prevailing epidemic, Rufus Tyler, Esq. Chief Coiner in the Branch Mint, and formerly of this town, aged 43.*
>
> *In the death of this enterprising man, the public has suffered a heavy loss, and his numerous friends , here and elsewhere experience the deepest affliction. They mourn Not, however as those without hope; for the departed one left behind him the consoling assurance of having exchanged this for a brighter world.*
>
> *In his last moments, he was cheered by the smile of his Savior as he entered the "dark valley" leaning upon an almighty arm.*
>
> *In death he was blest.*
>
>> *"When those we love are snatched away*
>> *By death's resistless hand,*
>> *Our hearts the mournful tribute pay*
>> *that friendship must demand.*
>>
>> *While pity prompts the rising sigh,*
>> *With awful power impress;*
>> *May this dread truth, "I too must die"*
>> *Sink deep in every breast.*
>> *Let this vain world allure no more;*
>> *Behold the op'ning tomb.*
>> *It bids us use the present hour,---*

Tomorrow death may come.
O! Let us to that Savior fly,
Who's arm alone can save;
Then shall our hopes ascend on high,
And triumph o'er the grave."

Bache was considered to be the leading American scientist of his day, so it isn't surprising that he was offered and took the position as Director of the U.S. Coast Survey (now NOAA). In that capacity, he reported to the Secretary of the Treasury Levi Woodbury. Robert Patterson also reported to Woodbury, so it's very likely Patterson recommended him for the position.

Bache continued as Director through six Presidents, and in 1862 during the Civil War, Lincoln tasked him with overseeing the defense of Philadelphia. Bache married his long time Secretary, but they never had any children. When his brother died, he adopted his brother's only child, HENRY WOOD BACHE, who also worked in the U.S. Coast Survey with him.

Alexander Dallas Bache died in 1867, leaving behind his wife and adopted son.

Henry Wood Bache married Eveline Coggeshall, and they had only one child, Eveline Coggeshall Bache. Eveline Coggeshall Bache never married and lived in Bristol Rhode Island all her life. When she died in 1955, she had no living heirs.

This brief history gives us the most likely explanation for what happened to the Tyler/Bache coin and note. When Bache received it from Rufus Tyler, the note remained wrapped around the coin, and it went into his family album which would have contained historic family letters as well as those sent to him.

About 1890, the value of rare mint marked coins (like the 1838-O half dollar) was becoming more generally known, and the coin would have been removed from the album for sale leaving behind the note. The coin was sold by dealer B.H.Collins to William Friesner, a West Coast businessman who specialized in collecting coins with mint marks.

When Friesner died, his collection was auctioned by Ed. Frossard on June 8/9, 1894 in New York, and the Cinderella coin was bought by Augustus Heaton. Heaton is considered the "father" of Mint Mark collecting, because of his 1893 book "A TREATISE ON COINAGE OF THE BRANCH MINTS OF THE UNITED STATES." Heaton was also the second president of the American Numismatic Association and had a great interest in the 1838-O half dollar which was featured prominently in his book. Once Heaton purchased the coin, he tried to find out where it had come from because of the great mystery surrounding its origin. He went back to Frossard, who went back to Collins, who went back to Eveline Bache. She was able to retrieve the Tyler note because it was still in the album. When Frossard got the note from Collins, he immediately recognized its importance and had it published in the July 1894 edition of The Numismatist. After that, he gave the note to Heaton, and that's the last time the famous note was ever seen, more than 120 years ago!

Granted, SOME of this is speculation, BUT it's the only reasonable way the note (a scrap of old paper) could survive and be recovered after being separated from the coin. If we can find the Bache family album, we can PROVE that this theory is true.

The search for the Bache family album is made much easier by their family tree which shows only a single line of heirs from Alexander Dallas Bache up to Eveline Coggeshall Bache, who was the last in that line.

I call the Bristol Rhode Island probate records office and request a copy of Eveline Coggeshall Bache's will.

They have it, and for a small fee they'll send me a copy.

The letter from Bristol Rhode Island arrives, and I open it with considerable anxiety. Will there be anything there, or will it be a dead end?

The will is a list of personal items Eveline has gifted to friends but nothing stands out. It IS a dead end, but there's one last page in a separate enclosed envelope. It reads "The Codicil to the will of Eveline Bache," and on page two it says "and to the Bristol R.I. Historical Society, I leave my valuable album with a letter from George Washington on the first page."

THIS is what I've been hoping for! It HAS to be the Bache family album, because that's the very first place anyone would put a letter from George Washington, and it was probably a congratulatory letter on the Marriage of Richard Bache to Benjamin Franklin's daughter or about Richard Bache's appointment as first Postmaster General. The good news is that there wouldn't be any more searching! Now I know EXACTLY where the album is.

Here is a challenge for all you would be treasure hunters! Please think about what else might be in a family album that traces its roots back to Benjamin Franklin. An album that was owned by the foremost American scientist of the first half of the nineteenth century and who was in the administrations of six different Presidents, from Polk to Lincoln. A man who travelled the world and knew the most famous people in Europe as well as the United States. Did you think about this? Many of the letters were probably put in the album while still in their envelopes, and this means that the album could contain one of the greatest troves of both autographs, letters and early American postage stamps ever found! THIS album is vastly more important and more valuable than the old scrap of paper we're looking for, and the ONLY evidence it ever even existed is a single line in the codicil of the will of someone with no living relatives. We've accidentally tripped over another treasure while searching for our lost letter!

I CAN'T WAIT to see this album, and I can't believe I've never heard of it already!

I call up the Bristol Historic Society, and I reach someone in charge.

"Hello, my name is Kin Carmody, and I'm doing some research on Eveline Coggeshall Bache."

"Yes! How can I help you?"

"I'd like to review her family album."

"Family album? I don't know anything about that."

I'm a bit surprised at that response given its obvious historical importance.

"You've NEVER hear of it? She willed it to the Bristol Historic Society in 1955, AND it has a letter from GEORGE WASHINGTON on the first page!"

"NO, but it MUST be in our Archives. Please give me your number and I'll call you back in a week after we've had a chance to look for it."

I thank him and hang up. I'm WAY beyond surprised. I'm STUNNED! The Historic Society has never even heard of what may be the most important set of American archival papers discovered in the past century! How could this even be possible?

I don't get a call back in a week, so after ten days I make a follow up call. Despite my intense desire to drop everything and go to Bristol, I don't want to press too hard, because these are the folks who are going to give me permission to actually look at the album.

I make the call and reach the same person I talked to previously.

"Yes. We checked, and we DON'T have the album. We had a fire around that time, and a lot of things were destroyed. The album you're looking for must have been lost in the fire."

"Do you have any records of having RECEIVED the album?" I ask.

"No. Those records were lost in the fire as well. Sorry we can't be of more help!"

I thank him again and hang up. This whole thing bothers me. There should have been some news about the bequest of an album with a letter from George Washington and there should have been some news about its loss.

On a whim, I call up the Bristol Fire Department.

"Yes! We have records of that fire. It was on the night of July 27, 1957 and let me see. Hmmm...it was ruled to be of SUSPICIOUS origin!"

In the spring of 1967, I returned home from college for a brief 3 day vacation after exams. My homecoming was always the same. I'd arrive at the front door and my mother would open it before I even rang the bell. She'd give me a hug while we were standing on the slate doorstep, which was surrounded by Lily of the Valley all in bloom with their white bells hanging down.

Then she would ALWAYS say "Your father is in the library waiting to see you!"

As you already know, my father was an austere man and THIS was my spring academic review with him.

I quickly took my suitcase upstairs to my room, opened it and came back down. My mother then ushered me into the library as always and closed the door behind me. The library was a small cedar paneled room lined with book shelves all filled with old weighty leather bound volumes. There were the complete works of Dickens, Sir Walter Scott, Stevenson, J.M. Barrie and many others, bound in reds, greens, browns and blues with gold lettering. There was a fireplace to the left with an antique brass screen and antique brass tools standing upright to the far side. My father sat in his favorite brown ancient leather chair which was lined with brass studs. The whole setting looked and felt like I'd stepped back in time.

The library had six tall leaded glass panel windows which could be opened with crank handles. It was a warm day, and all the windows were open even though there weren't any screens. It was spring, so the plague of black flies and mosquitos was still more than a month away. The windows overlooked my father's pool, which was more than a hundred feel across. It was a circular basin made out of white cement and he called it his "fire prevention pool," which helped with insurance because there weren't any fire hydrants within a mile of the house. The pool was ringed by a low stone wall and on the far side, it was bordered by a row of twenty perfectly symmetrical cypress. The pool was about twelve feet deep at its deepest spot, but it was only a foot deep at the edges making it easy for my mother to sit on the wall and then go in for her early morning swim. When the pool was first built five years earlier, my father had visions of stocking it with rainbow trout so he could go out and fly fish in the early mornings and evenings. I was tasked to catch minnows from the nearby lake to put into his pool as future trout food. I supplied the minnows but the trout never arrived, and by now the minnows were full fledged fish. My mother, on the other hand, had a contrary vision. SHE saw the pool as being filled with her fragrant pink and white pond lilies which she could enjoy during her morning and afternoon swims. I was tasked to "catch" the pond lilies from our old pond, which I also did. I planted the pond lilies in six large metal tubs, weighted them down with rocks and sank them at evenly spaced intervals. The pond lilies grew just as well as the minnows! In the movie "Field of Dreams" there's a very memorable line "If you build it, they will come!" That line applies to the ghosts of famous baseball players from long ago. It could ALSO apply to frogs snakes, turtles, raccoons and every other living creature within five miles. My parents built it, and they ALL came!

My father motioned for me to come in but not to sit. I would always remain standing while he reviewed my school record, which he held in his other hand. He began going through my courses and grades one by one and asked questions about each. I was used to the drill, and my grades were always good, so no worries! Suddenly, in the middle of one of his questions, he jumped up from his chair and hurried over to one of the open windows. There was a rifle propped up to one side that I hadn't noticed . He grabbed it, fired three quick shots at the pool and then leaned it back where it had been. He returned to his chair, picked up my transcript again and continued where he'd left off.

"Now, about this Mathematics class..."

I really wasn't listening any more. If he was THAT mad at the pool, he shouldn't have built it in the first place!

When his interrogation was over, he raised his right hand and gestured toward the door with two fingers. This was my dismissal, and It was time for me to leave. As I turned to open the library door he said,

"Say...you don't happen to still have your old mask and flippers upstairs do you?"

I didn't like where this line of interrogation was going! Being roasted alive for my grades was one thing, but THIS was something else altogether!

"Why do you ask?" I responded, knowing full well that I wouldn't like his answer, but at least it'd buy me some time.

"Well, a MONSTER snapping turtle has moved into the pond, and NOW your mother is afraid to go swimming . I thought you might put on your mask and flippers , if you still have them, and catch it!"

"OH" I said in a tone that weeped regret "UNFORTUNATELY they were thrown out years ago!"

After leaving the library, I headed straight up to my room and put my old mask and flippers securely in my suitcase. I'd just take them with me back to college. You never know when they might come in handy!

Some searches should NEVER be undertaken because you might just find what you're looking for! The pool was one and the Bristol fire is probably another. Finding the Tyler note would have been a great addition to the story, but it's a dead end now, so our focus has to return to the coin itself. Reaching dead ends and moving on will always be a part of internet treasure hunting.

Part 2
Cinderella Tells Her Story

The Great North Woods cover a million square miles from Northern Maine all the way to Hudson Bay. It's an endless tract of mountains, forests, rivers and lakes that harkens back to life a thousand years ago. In the mid summer of 1954, there were three log cabins set in a clearing back from the shore of Eagle Lake on the Allagash River in remote Northern Maine. The green asphalt shingle roofs and the dark brown creosoted cabin logs blended into the pine forest backdrop so the cabins were scarcely noticeable. There were no roads, no electricity, no telephones, no running water and not even a battery operated radio.The nearest outpost was the forest ranger station twenty miles away at the very end of the lake.

It was a life of hunting, fishing and cutting wood for cooking and the long bitterly cold winter months. I had just turned nine the week before, and one of my presents was a hunting knife with a sheaf that could be attached to my belt. It had rained hard the night before, so all the pine branches were drooping down from the weight of the moisture and the drops on the tips of the pine needles glistened in the early morning sun. If you brushed by one, you'd be as soaked as if you'd been caught out in a thunderstorm. My pants were soon wet up to my knees just from walking through the high grass across the clearing. A heavy rain at night is good for tracking, because animal tracks are so much clearer in the mud, and it's much easier to tell new tracks from old. That morning, my father told me to go far into the forest to look for deer tracks, because we hadn't seen any deer for several weeks. It would be a long hunt, because I was to go all the way past First Mountain and then go to the top of Second Mountain which would take at least 6 hours. Perfect days for tracking were rare, so this chance couldn't be missed. Today, such an adventure for a barely nine year old would be considered dangerous to the point of recklessness, but this was a different time in a different world. Any danger would be in the slippery rocks on the way to the mountain peak, and it would be foolish to venture close to the cliff edge. But if you grew up in that world at that time, you already knew about those kinds of dangers. The Spring and Fall were not times to venture into the forests alone, because of the dangers from mother bears with cubs and more aggressive male bears, but mid summer was safe. The bears were down at the rivers hunting for fish or in the lowlands among the wild blueberry bushes. I knew that too, and I had seen enough bear tracks so I could tell their size at a glance. I also knew not to take any food with me, because bears can smell it a mile away.

I filled my canteen and dressed in boots, long pants, long sleeved shirt and hat. The black flies are ferocious in mid July, and the oily repellent only does so much. I put rubber bands around my pant bottoms, tucked them inside my boots and then put rubber bands around my shirt cuffs...all this to keep the black flies and mosquitos from getting inside my clothing. With my new hunting knife securely on my belt, I set off through the woods behind the cabins. I followed an old game trail for about an hour. It was muddy and very slippery. There were no deer tracks here, but plenty of raccoon paw prints. Raccoons are drawn to our cabins by the left over food scraps and by the warmth underneath the floors. Living under one of our cabins during the winter is a far better deal than living in the middle of the forest. A heavy rain will flood out insects and worms and bring them to the surface, and it will water soak old rotten logs so they're easy to pull apart. There were several old rotten logs lying in pieces in the trail, broken apart by raccoons looking for grubs. Their tiny hand prints were perfectly preserved in the muddy path. It's way, way more than just looking at the signs on the ground. It's even more important to listen to the VOICE of the forest while you move forward as quietly and as silently as possible. Never step on a branch or a twig and carefully watch where you place your foot at every step. You want to pass through the forest as if you were a ghost, because this is THE ONLY WAY you can hear all the sounds of the forest. As soon a you make a noise, the forest goes silent. You can no longer hear the sounds you need to hear, and you're left with only the sound of your own breathing, your own heart beat and the light breeze in the trees.

Two hours on, there are still no deer tracks. Tiny mouse prints with their distinctive tail imprints trailing between are everywhere along with occasional red squirrel tracks, but they stay mainly up in the trees. The sounds of the forest fill the air, and it's important to sort them all out, otherwise they just blend into one ever present background noise. First, there are the insects...the cicadas high pitched scream, the buzz of *wasps coming and going and the ever present cloud of black flies close at hand. Above the insects are the birds...the occasional jay, crows in the distance and the drumming of a large pileated woodpecker on the upper reaches of a dead birch tree. High above, there will be the shrill cry of an eagle or a hawk on the hunt, and there's always the staccato burst of a scolding red squirrel. No matter how quietly you pass by, the red squirrel will always see you and chatter his warning to the rest of the forest. The blue jay will do the same, for these two, with their keen eyesight, are the guardians of the forest. As long as all these sounds continue in their current harmony, there's nothing amiss. When these sounds stop, then there's need to worry, because they never stop unless there's a very good reason.*

The game trail has long since split into dozens of other paths with no main one to follow. The trails still didn't show any large game tracks, but the one I now followed was etched in decades old marks on the trees rather than on the ground. The trail was marked years ago with "blazes" which are about fifty feet apart. Each blaze was marked at about 4 feet up on a tree trunk. It's made with a downward cut from a hatchet followed by a straight horizontal cut to remove the tree's bark to the size of a playing card. It's done on the front and back of each tree, so each one can be seen coming and going from the last blaze. New blazes are so white they're impossible to miss , but they become more difficult to see as their color fades over the years. If you've grown up in the woods, it's never a problem, because you know what to look for and where to look.

As I neared the top of Second Mountain, the trail became more vertical, clambering up boulders and crumbling embankments with the loose rocks and gravel giving way under my feet and clattering down below. There were no more blazes to follow, as the dirt was too shallow to support anything more than scrub trees. I had left the blazed trail behind to head up and I'd follow a giant loop coming back the other way to reconnect as I came down. I'd done this many times before, so there was no chance of getting lost. At the top, the scrub bushes gave way to open spaces of lichen covered granite slabs and finally out to the cliff face itself, with more than a hundred miles of the great north woods spread out before me. In the far distance were the pale blue twin peaks of Double Top Mountain, and in the near ground was all of Eagle Lake stretched out below. Forests, mountains and lakes as far as the eye could see and not another person or building in this pristine world of a long gone age. I took a long drink from my canteen and faced into the wind. I closed my eyes, felt the warm sun on my face and listened to the forest. I could feel and hear the wind, and I could feel the sun, but I couldn't hear the forest. When you stand by a waterfall or you're at the edge of a cliff, all the other sounds are buried. It was time to go back. I completed my loop, looking for the blaze that would mark my return to the trail home. Ten minutes down, and I spotted the aged marker, but something wasn't right. The blaze was right, the trail was right, but the forest was wrong! It was silent. No squirrels chattering, no drumming of woodpeckers, no random tweets of birds going about their daily routine. The insects were still buzzing their background noise but there was nothing else. I was on the path home because my bootprints from the trek up were clearly pressed into the mud. Everything that passes by, or follows, leaves a mark. That mark can be in the bent branches, in the overturned pebbles or in the mud. The marks were there, and even though I'd never seen them before, I knew immediately what they were, and it took my breath away. It's huge paw prints were in every one of my tracks, so large that they filled and even overlapped my boot marks. I unsheathed my hunting knife and quickly cut a five foot long moosewood sapling. It was about an inch in diameter, and it took no more than 30 seconds to sharpen its end to a wicked point...sharp but not brittle, so wouldn't break. It would have been better to temper the point in a fire, but there was no time for that. I doubled my pace back down the trail, with every one of my senses tingling. I was listening and looking, not just ahead, but side to side and especially behind and UP in the branches. And NO RUNNING! NEVER RUN! Running can trigger a predator's instinct to chase. I went off the trail to avoid all thickets and underbrush where ambush was possible and stayed in the open forest as much as possible. My knife would have been useless against the animal that was tracking me now.

The American Indians all know this. Every object in this world has two stories to tell. It tells the story of how it came to be, and it tells the story of all the things that have ever touched it. These stories are etched into the cracks and crevasses and even into the tiny chips of every rock. They've grown into the bark, the knots, the blazes and the broken limbs of every tree. They're even present in the slightly bent stalks and fronds of every blade of grass and every fern that carpets the forest floor. These stories are ALL there! You just have to know how to read them.

We've lost so much of that ability to read their stories, because we no longer take the time to look and to listen; to really closely look, and to really carefully listen! We no longer understand the writing that tells those stories nor do we recognize the marks we leave in our own passing. We each make so much noise that it becomes impossible to hear the sounds around us. Increasingly, we're all living in a cyberworld where there aren't any stories etched in the surfaces of cyber images, so there are no longer any real marks to read or real sounds to hear.

Since there's nothing left to read and nothing left to hear, there's no longer any need to look or to listen.

19

A Crack in the Case

IT'S TIME TO gather our treasure hunting team in our Cyber war room. I Truly believe that the Tyler/Bache coin is different from all the others, and it's something very special! That's what needs to be PROVEN, and from now on I'll call it THE CINDERELLA COIN until we have the final answer and know for certain its true identity. It's time for the Cinderella coin to tell her story, not through the archival letters that others have written, but through the marks and scars that are on the coin itself. How do we go about doing this? The first step is to identify all the characteristics of the coin that seem to be unique and seem to have some unexplained cause. Each of these has a story to tell. The second step is to try to read and decipher each one of those stories.

Here's the list for you to consider.

First, the Cinderella coin does NOT seem to have a die crack on the reverse that's common to all other known specimens.

Second, it has been heavily tarnished to the point of being nearly black because it was wrapped in a piece of high sulfur content paper for more than 50 years.

Third, it has marks on the reverse that seem to be consistent with the collapse of the reverse die, and these marks are not present on any other specimens.

Fourth, it seems to have a level of wear that the other specimens do not have. It has been suggested that this was "circulation wear," but this explanation is inconsistent with the fact that it was enclosed in the Tyler note from the time it was made until the time it was discovered.

Fifth, careful examination of the image details of the coin don't show any differences versus the image details on the other 8 specimens. The images are much less sharp and clear, but the images themselves seem to be identical.

Sixth, it doesn't seem to have any of the "proof" striking characteristics (mirrored surfaces, high reflectivity, sharp strike details) that are present on all the other specimens.

Seventh, it seems to have some kind of debris on the surface, especially in the cracks and crevasses of the images, that appears to be die rust.

THE GR-1 DIE CRACK

Dave Stone suggested I contact Dick Graham, the author of a book on "Reeded Edged Half Dollars" which included the 1838-O. Dick is recognized as the leading expert on these coins, and he gave me an invaluable lesson on "die cracks."

When coins were minted in the 1800's, a pair of dies were made out of steel. The front (obverse) had the impression of all the elements that would appear on the front of the coin, but they're in mirror image and recessed. Once the coin was struck, this image would appear raised and right side up. The same was true for the reverse die.

The obverse and reverse steel dies were then securely locked in place in a coin press, and the press could be operated continuously or to produce coins one at a time by hand. The striking pressure on the press could be varied, with greater pressure creating sharper, more detailed images. Circulation coins were produced in large numbers by continuous production, while "Proofs" were carefully produced one at a time under the highest striking pressure to make the sharpest possible image. The constant pounding of production inevitably took a toll on these early dies. They would wear down in places, and they would start to crack. Once a die cracked, it could still be used, but the crack would be imprinted on the coin as a raised line. The longer a cracked die was used, the longer the crack would become. On some early coins, the dies were so badly cracked that there was a spiderweb of lines across the front and reverse. These lines are called die cracks and don't diminish the value of the coin, because it's part of the minting process. The image below shows an extensive die crack that runs all the way around the perimeter of the coin.

Image courtesy of Heritage Auction Galleries

Dick Graham is the expert on the die crack that's present on the reverse of the 1838-O half dollar and on the reverse of most 1839-O half dollars (because the exact same reverse die was used for both years).

It's called the "GR-1" die crack, and it runs through the bottom lettering ("HALF DOL.") on the reverse. This die crack is hugely important because it's like tree rings. The longer the crack, the more recent the production of the coin. The smaller the crack, the earlier the production of the coin. The coin with the smallest GR-1 die crack would have to be the first minted, while the coin with the longest crack would have to be the last minted. Once the die crack is formed, it can never be reversed, so it's a proven measurement for determining the sequence of production.

The state of the GR-1 die crack on the Cinderella coin is a most important marker for revealing its story.

Heritage has excellent high resolution images of more than half of the 1838-O half dollars, and those images are a good starting point for studying the GR-1 die crack. The image on the left below shows the reverse of the "Atwater" specimen, and the raised die crack can be seen as a line that extends from beyond the first olive leaf, down through the letters "HALF DOL." The image on the right below shows the reverse of the Cinderella coin with no apparent die crack line. I spend more than an hour examining Cinderella under a high powered magnifying glass, and I still can't see any crack.

LOWER LEFT REVERSE
TYLER/BACHE NO
APPARENT DIE CRACK

LOWER LEFT REVERSE
ATWATER
GR- 1 DIE CRACK

Courtesy of Heritage Auction Galleries

The other specimens also show the die crack, so if Cinderella is the only one with no GR-1 die crack, then there are only two possibilities. Cinderella was struck first, before the die cracked, OR Cinderella was struck using a different uncracked reverse die.

THE BLACK TONING

We've already determined that the black discoloration on the coin is due to extreme toning or tarnishing due to being wrapped in a high sulfur content piece of paper for more than 50 years. Rufus Tyler, the author of the note, died of yellow fever on September 8, 1839, so he has to have placed the note around the coin very shortly after it was minted. It's also clear from Frossard's 1894 auction write up that the coin was discovered with the note still wrapped around it (about 1890-1892). A close examination shows that the black toning is ON TOP of both the reverse distress marks and the apparent "circulation wear" that's reduced the sharpness of the image details on the coin.

This has to mean that BOTH the reverse marks AND the lack of image detail were in place on the coin BEFORE it was wrapped in the note. This effectively means that both of these features were a result of the striking process and not of outside factors that occurred at a later time. By way of example, if you take one of my burned pennies from my first grade birthday party and rub it, you'll start to remove the black. The place you rub will go to dark brown, to light brown and eventually back to copper. There is no evidence that this happened on the device details or around the reverse marks. However, there IS the slightest indication of the black toning being worn around the tip of Liberty's chin and nose. THIS shows that some minimal high point wear did occur and it's completely consistent with the coin sliding back and forth inside its paper note if it had been stored in an album.

The available evidence on the surface of the coin PROVES that the reverse marks were made by the collapse of the reverse die support system that Tyler referenced in his letter of Feb 25, 1839 rather than by some other outside agent at a later time.

The marks form a series of gouges in the metal that extend in a perfect circular arc for more than 17% of the circumference of the coin. This arc has the exact same curvature, radius and arc length as the underlying reverse die.

The gouges line up perfectly with the raised dentils on the rim of the reverse die, and the marks made are exactly what one would expect to see if the reverse die moved across the edge of the coin with some horizontal force vector.

THE MARKS ON THE REVERSE

Courtesy of Heritage Auction Galleries

The black toning is ON TOP of these marks proving that they had to have been made during, or immediately after production.

Any outside agent striking the coin with enough force to cause those gouges would also cause severe friction marks on the other side of the coin. For example, pick up any coin you find in the street and turn it over. The damage to the side that's down and suffers the friction is always greater than the side that's run over by the cars.

There is absolutely no friction damage on the other side of the coin, so that means that it had to have been locked in place in the coin press when the reverse marks were made.

THE WEAK IMAGE DETAIL ON THE COIN

Courtesy of Heritage Auction Galleries

As you can see from the images above, the image details on the Cinderella coin are much less sharp and are more "blurred" than the details on the Eliasberg specimen. All the other specimens have very sharp images, with the Cinderella coin being the only exception. Here again, there are a number of facts that prove the lack of strike detail is due to the minting process.

The lack of detail is UNDERNEATH the black toning, so circulation wear is not a possibility.

The lack of detail is most pronounced on the lower parts of the design elements rather than the upper parts. Circulation wear ALWAYS occurs starting with the highest points of a design element and progresses down with increased wear. A weak strike shows the strongest details at the top of a design element and the weakest at the bottom due to the lack of striking pressure. This is exactly the case with the Cinderella coin as can best be seen in the tips of the stars on the obverse. The design lines across the highest point of the stars are clearly defined, but the points of the stars taper downward and practically disappear at the ends. It's as if the stars points are not completely formed. This can't be caused by wear, because the tips are the lowest part of the star. The conclusion that this is due to a weak strike is also confirmed when the Cinderella coin is viewed "edge on" showing that the entire strike and all the design elements are extremely shallow.

This Isn't very surprising given that Tyler's February 25, 1839 letter states that the reverse die was "spliced" into place because it was too short to be properly and firmly secured. This means it's almost certain that Tyler would have used very low striking pressure on his "jury rigged" system. All the other specimens were made under very high PROOF striking pressure, so we can conclude that the other specimens could not have been struck in the same early Jan 1839 run as the Cinderella coin.

NO DIFFERENCES IN IMAGE DESIGN

A close comparison of all the design elements across different specimens doesn't show any meaningful differences. Even the "hand punch" elements such as the date, the stars and the lettering all seem to be in the same relative positions on the obverse and reverse. This means that all known specimens were struck from the same pair of dies OR that a second set of dies was used that was an EXACT match of the first set. This is very unlikely, but not totally impossible.

LACK OF PROOF CHARACTERISTICS

The Cinderella coin doesn't have any of the primary features associated with a PROOF coin. It doesn't have sharp image details due to high striking pressure, and it doesn't have highly reflective surfaces that are associated with the proof polishing of both the dies and the blank coin planchettes before they were fed into the coin press. All the other specimens have these proof characteristics. This is further evidence that the other coins could not have been struck during the first run on Tyler's jury rigged system. It couldn't have achieved the required strike pressure for PROOF images, and the coins from that short 10 coin run would all have the same striking characteristics. Clearly, they do not. Cinderella is the one exception.

It should be noted that for more than a hundred years the 1838-O half dollar has been considered a "PROOF ONLY" issue based on expert examination of all specimens EXCEPT The Cinderella coin. This one specimen has never been closely examined by anyone, and it was assumed to be a PROOF, because all the other 1838-O's were proofs. Its lack of proof features has always been attributed to "circulation wear," but we now know that isn't the case.

APPARENT DIE RUST ON THE SURFACE OF CINDERELLA

The presence of what appears to be die rust on the surface of the Cinderella coin was first pointed out by David Stone and Mark VanWinkle in their booklet "THE SURPRISING HISTORY OF THE 1838-O HALF DOLLAR." This is a critical issue, because IF the Cinderella coin was made from a pair of rusted dies, then it's almost certain that all the other specimens were made as PROOFS in Philadelphia, and that the same dies were then shipped to New Orleans where they rusted in storage. This is the primary contention in their booklet.

The enlarged image of the Cinderella coin below shows the bluish green residue that may be die rust. The residue is most obvious in and around the date and in the recessed areas of the image.

Courtesy of Heritage Auction Galleries

The primary problem with the "die rust" theory is that the distribution of this residue doesn't follow the typical pattern that would be seen with a rusted die. This pattern is more like what would happen if a fine powder was blown across the surface and got caught in the nooks and crannies of the coin.

At this point, it's important to understand the chemical process involved in die rust. Coin dies are made from STEEL, so they're much harder than the silver coins they strike. Steel doesn't rust the same way Iron rusts. When Iron rusts, it forms "IRON OXIDE," which is Fe 2 O3. When steel rusts, it forms "IRON HYDROXIDE" which is Fe2 (OH) 3. This difference is very important because IRON HYDROXIDE is known as "GREEN RUST" and has the exact same blue/green color as the residue on the surface of the Cinderella coin. This can't be just a coincidence, since there are no other examples of this residue appearing on other silver coins, and the Cinderella coin was wrapped in note paper for most of its existence which would have protected it from some unusual contamination. This means that the residue was almost certainly a result of the minting process, but whether it's due to rusted dies is an open question.

These are the stories we can get from the marks on the coin and they all represent new pieces to the puzzle, BUT I'm not a recognized expert in Numismatics. I'm actually a complete unknown novice in Numismatics, so NO ONE is going to take any of my conclusions seriously. They'll all have to be vetted and confirmed by an unimpeachable outside source.

20

Alignment of the Stars Solves the 1838-O Mystery!

I CALL DAVE STONE to tell him about my latest discoveries. He listens with great patience, and then he drops a bombshell! Two of the leading Numismatic experts in the U.S. have just published a book titled "ALIGNMENT OF THE STARS," and it answers ALL the questions about the 1838-O half dollar. The authors are highly respected, and their book is 100 pages long. It includes ALL the information available, copies of every known archival letter relating to these coins, images of all known specimens as well as a detailed analysis by other experts including the world's leading authority on REEDED-EDGE half dollars dated 1836-1839.

They have finally solved the 1838-O half dollar mystery! Their conclusions end my hope that "THE CINDERELLA COIN" is the only one actually minted in New Orleans. They PROVE that no specimens were ever minted in Philadelphia and that all known specimens, except for one, were struck in the first run in New Orleans in January 1839. The one exception is the coin in the Smithsonian collection, which was especially struck in late March /early April, 1839 for the Mint collection at Patterson's request. It has been in the collection ever since.

What can I say? The search is over.

"Dave, do you have a copy, and have you read their book yet?"

"No...but I talked to one of the authors last week and he gave me this top line summary. Sorry if it's bad news!"

"It is what it is. Thanks for the posting Dave."

It's clear that my treasure hunt is over now. The authors of this book are two of the most respected Numismatists in the world, and they have access to research and letters that I've never even heard of.

Many years ago when my daughter Lindsey first started teaching 5th grade, I used to send her e mails, which she'd read to her class. Sometimes they were informative, sometimes they were funny and sometimes they were both. I sent her the following email on March 31.

"Hi Lindsey. There's a REALLY BIG ASTRONOMICAL EVENT that's going to occur tomorrow morning at 10:48. Have you heard about it? It's a once in a lifetime thing, and you really don't want to miss it! At exactly 10:48am tomorrow morning, there will be a "FULL OCCLUSION OF THE SUN." This is an EXTREMELY rare event that takes place when the sun passes between the earth and the moon. What's even rarer is that for the first time in 500 years, the "full occlusion" will actually take place during the day!"

Despite some pretty obvious problems with my description, Lindsey had her entire class outside with dark glasses waiting for the magic moment of their brief lifetimes to arrive. They were all lined up like a town full of prairie dogs scanning the sky for predators. After checking their watches several times, one especially bright 5th grader noted that Lindsey was nowhere to be seen, and it WAS April fool's day. A mere coincidence no doubt, but as time went on, that seemed to be less and less likely. The very next year on April 1, Lindsey arrived to her classroom at 7am to find that every single item not bolted to the floor was gone, and NOTHING was bolted to the floor. This disappearance was a total mystery to her former class who were now 6th graders. They suggested that it MIGHT

have been caused by a "full occlusion" of her classroom...an
EXTREMELY rare event, but stranger things have happened!

Just because something is written down in an email (or a book) doesn't automatically make it true. I need to buy a copy of ALIGNMENT OF THE STARS and read it myself.

I get the phone number for one of the authors and call up to order a copy. A week later the book arrives with a brief handwritten note on the bottom right corner of the first page.

"Kin, hope you enjoy!" ENJOY was not exactly the word that came to mind given the bad news, but I knew I'd find it extremely interesting, because I'd finally get to see all the pieces to this puzzle and how they all fit together. The very next day I begin reading.

"Acknowledgements." This section contains a list of all the expert contributors to their 100 page book along with their resumes, and there are enough names to sink a battleship. Dave Stone and Mark VanWinkle's names are even on the list for the work they'd done in their booklet "The Surprising History of the 1838-O Half Dollar." Everyone who was anyone was included. Even people who weren't anyone were mentioned. This was going to be an extremely thorough and well researched work with no holes or weak points whatsoever!

"Foreword." Page 5 is the "foreword," and things don't get any more encouraging.

The summary reads;

"The discovery of new information regarding the 1838-O half dollar that ABSOLUTELY answers many of the most important questions such as WHEN these varieties were struck; WHERE they were struck; WHICH coins were struck in which striking; WHY they were struck; WHO struck them, and so on."

Oh well! There is some good news in all of this. The 1838-O half dollar IS important enough for the leading experts to do all this research and then write a 100 page book about it. The bad news is that the Cinderella coin isn't a Princess at all and can't be called "THE CINDERELLA COIN" anymore.

I continue reading and come to the two most important pieces to this puzzle that I'd been missing.

First, they had found a letter in the National Archives that said that the 1838-O dies were unfinished and in an "unhardened" state when they were shipped to New Orleans. This was done to prevent their use in case they were stolen. It isn't possible to strike coins using unhardened and unfinished dies. Both the finishing and hardening was done in New Orleans. That's a torpedo in my theory that the Cinderella coin is the only one actually made in New Orleans. They were ALL made in New Orleans!

The second new piece of information was even more surprising. Famed Numismatist, John Dannreuther, had gone to the Smithsonian museum and personally examined their specimen that had been in the Mint collection since 1839. His analysis of the GR-1 die crack on that specimen proved that it had been made AFTER several 1839-O proof half dollars, and it showed a bigger , more developed , die crack than all other 1838-O's. Since the New Orleans Mint didn't receive any 1839 dies until mid March 1839 and there was no operational half dollar press until March 27,1839, this analysis proves that the Smithsonian specimen was made on or after March 27, 1839. Dannreuther has proven that there was a second striking of 1838 half dollars in New Orleans that was previously unknown and for which there is absolutely no written record. There are no archival letters of any kind that even hint at this second run, even though we now know it took place. "Alignment of the Stars" concludes that Mint Director Patterson must have requested a PROOF sample for his Mint cabinet collection, and THAT was the reason for this previously unknown striking. They also conclude that as many as 5 PROOF coins were probably produced in this second striking, but four of those have been lost along with Patterson's letter asking that the coins be made and sent.

The next section of "Alignment of the Stars" contains a detailed analysis of each of the 9 known specimens along with images and conclusions.

I read on, studying every picture and every word.

21

Trouble Right Here in River City!

"**ALIGNMENT OF THE STARS**" states that the Smithsonian specimen was made on, or shortly after, March 27, 1839. All other 8 known specimens were made in the original January 1839 striking that ended when the support system for the reverse die collapsed. My coin is one of those made in the original run. All 8 of these "originals" are part of a clearly defined sequence, and it's possible to determine the exact order of their production by studying the extent of the GR-1 die crack on the reverse of each coin. There are images that show the details of the obverse and reverse of each one. Their analysis virtually proves that all the coins (including the Smithsonian) were struck using the same pair of dies, which makes sense to me. I had spent hours trying to find the slightest difference in the details of the arrows, eagle feathers , hair strands, stars and letters in order to show that The Cinderella Coin had been struck using a different obverse or reverse die, but I had come up empty. There were NO differences, so the same dies must have been used for all the coins. Since no 1838-O half dollars could have been minted in Philadelphia because the dies were unusable, and since all 9 specimens were minted in New Orleans using the same pair of dies, it looks like the end of the road for our treasure hunt! At least I still have our PROVENANCE!

I was named after my Grandfather, Edward Kinsley, and I guess that means I'm supposed to inherit all his best qualities, but that isn't true. When I was little, Mother would say to her friends "Kinsley's grandfather was SUCH a wonderful singer! Did you know he used to sing in the choir? He had SUCH a beautiful voice! Everyone said so. Kinsley has a beautiful voice just like his grandfather, and some day HE will sing in the choir."

This was repeated so many times, I knew it by heart.

One day, when I was 10, I came home from school, and I went up to my room to play. I was softly singing to myself "on top of ol' smoky, all covered with snow." I only knew that first line, but I liked it, so I just sang it over and over again. Once my door was closed, my singing got louder and louder. "On top of OL' SMOKY, all covered with snow! On top of OL' SMOK...EEEE.."

I heard my mother scream from the kitchen and then come running up the stairs. She threw open the door.

"Are you hurt? Are you all right?" she cried, almost out of breath.

"I just fell down, but I'm OK now." I lied.

The next year I was accepted at Groton School, a boarding school that would be my home for the next six years. I'd start in the fall of 1958 in the seventh grade which was called First Form. Mother was MOST excited for me!

"Groton has a choir! Kinsley WILL sing in their choir because he has SUCH a wonderful voice. He gets it from his grandfather. His grandfather sang in the choir, and he had a wonderful voice! Everyone said so!"

The choir at Groton had a certain order and structure that was every bit as important as the sound that came out of it. There were two banks of pews on either side of the alter with an equal number of seats on each side. Each bank was made up of rows that got progressively higher. In the very bottom row were the sopranos, in the next were the altos, and the deepest voices were in the top row. Since Groton had six grades going from 7th to 12th, the 7th graders were needed to fill the soprano sections in the bottom rows because our voices hadn't changed yet. By sheer coincidence, there were exactly 12 soprano seats (6 on the bottom right and 6 on the bottom left), and the first form ALWAYS admitted exactly 12 students; never more and never less.

It was the fall of 1958, and it was time for choir "tryouts." While 8th graders and older actually had a choice and had to be selected to make the choir, all 7th graders were forceably conscripted. For us, "trying out" was not a voluntary thing. I had no illusions whatsoever about my voice and absolutely dreaded the audition. I went to Mr. Gammons, the choir master and music teacher, and desperately pleaded to get out of it.

"No! Every 7th grader has ALWAYS tried out for the choir, and EVERY SINGLE ONE has made it!" He said, reassuringly.

"Can I audition in private?"

"Nonsense! Your mother tells me you have a WONDERFUL voice! She tells me you get it from your grandfather."

DOOMED! I was looking forward to this about as much as King Louie XVI was looking forward to his execution. The try outs were held in Mr. Gammon's music room and not in the chapel, and the room was packed. I was going to have my chance to sing in front of ALL my 7th grade classmates, who would never ever let me forget. I would be in front of the 8th graders who would use this as one more form of torture, and I would be in front of all the upper class, who would forever use this as a form of branding.

One by one my classmates stood up, went to the front of the room, turned and faced Mr. Gammons for their turn.

My time came at last, and I felt like I was in the wooden wheeled cart of the French Revolution moving ever closer to the Guillotine. Finally, I mounted the stairs and turned to face my executioner, knowing that my song would be my very last words.

It was over in an instant, and it was mercifully quick! Mr. Gammons dropped his baton like the falling blade of the guillotine, and my singing was cut off in mid sentence. The look on his face was one of both astonishment and great pain.

"N-NEXT!" he stammered, clearly trying to move on as quickly as possible and hoping that the assembled audience was hard of hearing or had a very short memory. When I returned to my seat, I kept my eyes firmly fixed on the floor so I didn't have to look at anyone.

There were exactly 12 seats in the two soprano rows and exactly twelve 7th graders. It was impossible to take an 8th grader whose voice was still soprano and put him into the lowest soprano row to fill a seat. THAT would have caused a riot with major bloodshed by the 8th graders with all us 7th graders as their victims. While not encouraged, such riots were a regular part of lower school life, but rioting and bloodshed in the chapel itself was generally frowned upon. It wasn't an option to leave one of the soprano seats vacant either, because THAT would send a clear message that there wasn't even enough interest in the choir to fill all its seats. Then, that most unfortunate message would have been broadcast to the entire community every day and twice on Sunday when chapel was held.

No...THAT would never do! There was only one solution. The next day Mr. Gammons came up to me and said;

"CONGRATULATIONS! You're in the choir." He then leaned in a bit closer, and in his lowest possible voice said.

"NEVER let a sound pass your lips!"

So, I WAS in the choir, but I WASN'T supposed to sing. I was to be a "silent partner" so to speak. It seemed to me that there might be some possible upside in my humiliation after all.

"Since I'm not going to sing, do I STILL have to go to choir practice?" Choir practice was a real pain in the butt. It lasted more than an hour for at least 3 times a week, AND that didn't include going to chapel early 8 times a week and practice immediately before and after Sunday services.

"YES!" Mr. Gammons said, and then added *"Everyone MUST go to choir practice."*

"WHY do I have to go, if I'm not going to sing?"

Mr. Gammons thought about this for a bit.

"You have to go because you'll get better at holding your hymnal and moving your lips. You'll get better at LOOKING like you're singing."

I thought about THAT for a bit. I was going to invent "lip sinc" in 1958. Who knew!

"IF I get really good at it, can I do a SOLO?"

Mr. Gammons didn't think very long about that idea at all.

"NO," he said *"THAT would NOT be a very good idea?"*

"Why not?"

"BECAUSE it would make a mockery of the choir AND my entire life's work!"

I thought about that and decided he was probably right, and the whole thing would most likely end with even more humiliation.

Mr. Gammons was very thoughtful and even gave me a special seat in the soprano section. I was in the very last seat all the way to the end. I was as far away from the congregation as possible and as close to the organ pipes as possible, and dressed in my red and white robes, I looked just like every other member of the choir.

Mother was SO PROUD! She told all her friends.

"Kinsley made the Groton choir! I KNEW he would. You know he gets it from his grandfather. His grandfather sang in the choir, and he had a wonderful voice. EVERYONE said so!"

Just because something looks the same doesn't mean it is.

I continue reading the section in "Alignment" on the reverses of the 1838-O half dollars and their GR-1 die cracks. They show an image of my coin, the Anderson DuPont specimen, and write under reverse diagnostics;

"NONE NOTED." That means they don't see any sign of the GR-1 die crack on the reverse of my coin, and they also write;

"NOTE: As this coin has signs of wear, it is possible that the (GR-1) die cracks used as diagnostics are worn away."

"I DON'T THINK SO!" I say to myself. For the first time since I started reading, I feel a bit of doubt. "Wear" on a coin doesn't work that way. The highest points are always THE FIRST to wear, not the lowest points on the surface, and the die crack was certainly at the lowest point. The lowest points, like the die crack, are THE LAST to wear.

Under the "Atwater" specimen, they also write about the GR-1die crack;

"NONE NOTED"

All the other specimens show the GR-1die crack.

This comparison allows "Alignment" to conclude that the Atwater specimen was the first coin produced in the original January, 1839 production sequence and Anderson DuPont was the second. Since my coin was in between other coins that were part of the sequence, then it HAD TO BE PART OF THE SEQUENCE AS WELL.

This is a completely logical and understandable conclusion, except for one problem. I had studied the "Atwater" specimen extensively when I'd done my comparison, and there are two excellent images of the coin on the Heritage website. The largest image doesn't show any crack, and that's the image ALIGNMENT used. However, there's a smaller image of ATWATER in its coin holder, and THAT IMAGE shows a highly developed and strongly defined GR-1 die crack. When the pictures are taken, the angle of the light can cause the crack to stand out or disappear completely. Anderson DuPont is the ONLY specimen with no apparent die crack, so it's not necessarily in their sequence. If it IS in their sequence, then it would have to be the very first one produced, because it has the least developed GR-1 die crack.

In a following section, Alignment of the Stars presents, and then refutes, alternative theories about the origin of the 1838-O half dollar, and THERE IT IS! Theory Number 7 (on page 47) "The Anderson DuPont 1838-O half dollar was the only coin struck at the New Orleans Mint." In refuting this theory which I've been trying so hard to prove, they write the following about my poor misunderstood coin.

"It was believed that this coin had evidence of die rust on the reverse. Die rust or corrosion would normally cause pitting in the face of the die, which would show up as raised lumps on the coin struck. The raised lumps on this specimen are simply the result of dirt and other material building up on the coin especially around the design elements during circulation. It was the pattern of dust, not the pattern of die rust. None of the other surviving 1838-O half dollars have any indication of rust, which should be the first indication that this was not the result of rust."

This is ALL TRUE, but my analysis also suggests that my coin had very little circulation, AND the blue green color of the "dirt" is virtually unique to steel rust.

I continue reading, and Alignment addresses the marks on the reverse of the Anderson DuPont specimen. They write on page 48 "There are also several half arches protruding from the denticles on the bottom of the Anderson DuPont specimen underneath "Half " and "Do" of "Dol." It is unknown what caused these images. It may be some kind of build up caused when the coin was in circulation. The best way to determine if this is part of the coin or added after is to examine the coin outside the slab (holder)."

And finally they write;

"There are diagnostics, such as die cracks on the 1838-O half dollars that clearly show the sequence in which these coins were struck. It can be shown through diagnostics that other 1838-O half dollars were struck before the Anderson DuPont specimen and a progression of diagnostics that show which coins were struck after."

They make a very strong argument, but I'm not 100% convinced.

The unique characteristics of my coin are too quickly dismissed as dust, debris and photographic distortion, and their sequence argument Isn't valid given the other image of the Atwater specimen.

When Lindsey was little, her two favorite games were "Candy Land" and "Old Maid." Patti and I were playing Candy Land with her one day, and all our counters were merrily marching around the board without the slightest hint of any bad luck in drawing an unfortunate card. After the game was over, I looked through all the cards and found that she had removed every single bad one. That wasn't enough! To make absolutely certain that those bad cards would never rear their ugly heads again, she cut them all up into little pieces. I checked the Old Maid game too, and the "Old Maid" was nowhere to be found. Away on vacation no doubt!

So here it is. ALIGNMENT says there really IS a die crack on the Cinderella coin. You just can't see it because it's worn away. There is no die rust. It's just blue green dirt from circulation. There are no reverse marks from the collapsed reverse die. This is just more circulation dirt, but a different color this time. The Anderson DuPont specimen is in the Middle of the run because the Atwater coin doesn't show any die crack.

ALIGNMENT CLEARLY STATES THAT THEIR CONCLUSIONS ARE BASED ON IMAGES FROM COINS IN THEIR HOLDERS, AND THIS CAN BE MISLEADING! The best analysis should always be done out of the holder by experts. This is EXCELLENT advice which I'll take, but I feel a bit like someone has taken all the bad cards out of the 1838-O game and cut them up to make them fit.

22

Yet Another Monday with Morris

WE'RE AT THE Oakridge Pub for our last Monday night hamburger dinner before we leave for the summer, and Morris wastes no time with pleasantries. He cuts right to the chase.

"So, how's the treasure hunt going?"

I need to quickly counter his verbal sword thrust with a deft parry of my own.

"So, how's the GOLF game going?"

"I'm STILL thinking of giving it up. I'm not getting any better. Are YOU thinking of giving up your treasure hunt?"

Morris is very sharp tonight, with another lunge right to my heart, but I sidestep his blade and counter with a feint of my own.

"NOT AT ALL! Things are going almost swimmingly!" I don't even know what that means, but I'm hoping Morris doesn't either, so he'll drop his guard in a state of confusion.

Morris DOESN'T drop his guard.

"What do you mean ALMOST swimmingly?" He replies.

I'm now on the defensive.

"WELL, I've had a MINOR setback. Nothing to speak of really...BUT, I've also had an absolutely STUNNING SUCESS!"

I'm back on the attack!

"I've PROVEN that my coin is the very same one that had the famous Tyler Note wrapped around it and was auctioned in 1894. THAT means I've PROVEN its PROVENANCE all the way back to the Chief Coiner who made the coin in 1839. NGC, one of the leading grading and certification companies, has OFFICIALLY approved my claim and will re label the holder as soon as I submit it. It will be known as the "TYLER/BACHE" specimen from now on!"

Morris is impressed but hasn't put his sword down quite yet.

"That IS good news! What's the incredibly MINOR setback you ran into?"

I decide to ignore his vain attempt to regain the offense and choose to continue my line of attack.

"As far as I know, there isn't any other rare American coin that can trace its history all the way back to the person who made it. This is a TREMENDOUS breakthrough, and it should increase its value substantially!"

"And the MINOR setback?" Morris asks again. I'll say this for Morris. He's nothing if not persistent. He can be a regular bulldog when he wants to be. This time I HAVE to answer.

"There are two people who've just published a book on the 1838-O half dollar, and they CLAIM to have solved the mystery. This means that I'll probably stop doing any more research."

Morris' reaction isn't what I expected.

"REALLY! They wrote an ENTIRE BOOK on your coin? That's AMAZING! I had no idea it was THAT important!"

"Yes. It was just published, and it's more than a hundred pages long. It really has all the information there is in the world on the 1838-O half dollar, and the authors are extremely well respected experts, so there's probably not a lot I can add. I have a copy of their book, and I'm reading it now."

Our duel appears to be over, so we put down our swords and attack our dinners instead. I won't see Morris again until the fall, when we return from Cape Cod.

23

Trouble Gets Much Worse in River City

THE MORNING AFTER my dinner with Morris, I continue reading ALIGNMENT OF THE STARS, but with a little bit more of a skeptical eye.

It's important to understand the context of the times in New Orleans in 1839, when the 1838-O half dollars were minted. In 1839, it's unlikely there were any serious coin collectors in the New Orleans area. The hobby was in its infancy, and what few collectors there were lived in the Philadelphia/New York area in proximity to the Philadelphia Mint. There was NO collecting of "mint marked" coins made by the branch mints for the very obvious reason that the very first branch mints in the U.S. didn't start production until 1838. In fact, it wasn't until the publication of "A Treatise on coins of the Branch Mints of the United States" by Augustus Heaton in 1893 that Mint Mark collecting became popular among Numismatists. His book catalogued the relative rarity of the different Mint Mark issues, and Augustus Heaton became known as "the father" of Mint Mark collecting.

Between 1839 and 1860 there were times when the silver content of half dollars was worth more than the face value of the coins and this resulted in the melting of many of the coins.

Finally, there was the devastating Civil War on the economy of the South. Confederate paper money became virtually worthless, so gold and silver coinage was at a premium. If you were desperate to buy necessities, any coins available would have been used even if they were part of a collection.

I continue to read with this perspective in mind.

Alignment PROVES that the first original production run was to MAKE COINS FOR CIRCULATION because they include a letter from the National Archives dated January 17, 1839 from Mint Director Robert Patterson to New Orleans Mint Superintendent ordering production to start up.

> *"It appears to me that no time should be lost in getting ready for the coinage of half dollars. Dimes and half dimes count too slowly, and keep your amount of coinage too low."*

I CAN'T argue with that conclusion! ALIGNMENT PROVES that 10 coins were struck for circulation before the reverse die support system collapsed ending the run because they include the well known letter dated February 25, 1839 from Chief Coiner Rufus Tyler to Mint Director Patterson that describes the run and subsequent failure.

> *"...the bottom ones (reverse dies) are too short to reach the screws and consequently cannot be secured in the seats. I have however spliced one of them in order to try the press and succeeded in making ten excellent impressions, the very first ones struck being as perfect as the dies, are entirely satisfactory, but the piece upon the bottom of the die became loose, and I was unable to strike any more without fixing,"*

On page 44 of ALIGNMENT OF THE STARS, Dannreuther and Flynn write "If the support system had not failed under the half dollar working dies in the large coining press, Tyler would have most likely continued striking half dollars, and these coins would then not be rare. It can be clearly shown that the intended method and intent of manufacture was to strike half dollars for circulation."

It so happens that I have a copy of this letter sent directly from the National Archives, and there are a couple of points that need to be emphasized and clarified.

First, "ten" is UNDERLINED in Tyler's letter indicating that EXACTLY 10 coins were struck for circulation. Not more and not less.

Second, this letter means that Mint Director Patterson KNEW that the New Orleans had exactly 10 1838-O circulation strikes in its possession.

Third, the transcription of the line "the very first ONES struck being as perfect as the dies themselves, ARE entirely satisfactory," should read "the very first ONE struck being as perfect as the dies themselves, AND entirely satisfactory," This means that ONLY THE VERY FIRST COIN STRUCK WAS ENTIRELY SATISFACTORY. In other words, Tyler saw some problems or defects with all the others after the first one that made them less than completely acceptable.

This letter also leaves unanswered the question as to whether Tyler FIXED the large press at a later date and ran more 1838-O half dollars.

Finally, Alignment proves that once Patterson received Tyler's letter of February 25 describing the failed run, he ordered that no more 1838-O half dollars be produced. They include this archival letter dated March 15, 1839 from Patterson to Superintendent Bradford.

"I advise that the dies of 1838 BE NOT USED BY YOU, that we have sometimes used the dies of a particular year for a few days after it's close."

The most important thing about THIS letter is that the order is such a total one. There was to be NO MORE production of 1838 half dollars for any reason whatsoever...NOT for circulation and NOT for Proof samples either! His order was so direct that Superintendent Bradford felt obliged to IMMEDIATELY IMPLEMENT PATTERSON'S ORDER and respond back to him as soon as possible.

Alignment includes this letter from Bradford to Patterson dated March 29, 1839.

"Your letters of the 14th and 15th inst (of this month) are before me. The pair of half dollar dies (the first receipt of 1839 dated dies) which you sent on the 12th have also arrived.

I stated to Mr. Tyler that you advised that the dies of 1838 BE NOT USED and I suggested that it would be best to return them to you, thinking they might serve some purpose, but he thought it not worthwhile. I have to request that you give me such directions in relation to the dies of 1838 now in hand in this Branch Mint as the case requires.

I have the pleasure of informing you that Mr. Tyler has got the half dollar coining press in operation. He commenced striking on the evening of the 27th inst (of this month) and the press is now performing admirably."

There are THREE important things to note about this letter.

First, the topics appear to be covered in sequential order as they occurred, rather than in order of importance. Bradford received the 1839 dies, Bradford told Tyler about Patterson's order, Bradford is concerned about the handling of 1838 dated assets and Tyler started half dollar production on the evening of March 27.

Second, it is clear that Bradford had great concern over the accounting for, and the disposition of, the materials relating to the now prohibited 1838 half dollar dies and coins. This isn't surprising given Patterson's well deserved reputation for extreme detail management and the accounting for all Government assets under his authority.

Third, the production start up of the half dollar press on the EVENING of March 27 seems very unusual as this would have meant production well into the night with few people available to assist. March 27, 1839 was a Wednesday (middle of the week) so not much would have been lost by starting on the following morning.

Overall, I completely agree with the conclusions reached by

Alignment in this section. They've done a masterful job in pulling all the evidence together. The archival letters PROVE that exactly 10 1838-O half dollars were struck for circulation in January 1839 on the large dollar press and that production of 1839-O half dollars began on the half dollar press on the evening of March 27, 1839.

The next section of Alignment has three main conclusions:

First, NO 1838-O half dollars were ever made in Philadelphia.

Second, the circulation strikes produced in New Orleans in the original January, 1839 were handed out locally by Tyler and/or Bradford as souvenirs, and there are 8 survivors from this 10 coin run.

Third, the Smithsonian specimen, along with 4 or 5 other PROOFS, were struck on the evening of March 27 or later on the half dollar press in New Orleans. These specimens were made specifically for Mint Director Patterson at his request for inclusion into his Mint Cabinet collection, and there is just 1 survivor (the coin in the collection).

Their evidence for these conclusions is as follows:

None could have been struck in Philadelphia because the dies were unfinished and unhardened when they were shipped to New Orleans. It is admitted in a footnote that it is possible (but unlikely) that a pair of dies could have been hardened for production of proofs in Philadelphia and then re-softened for shipment to New Orleans.

There is only one documented striking of 1838-O half dollars and that's the January 1839 circulation run in New Orleans, so the coins HAD to have been made at that time. 8 of the 9 survivors are from that run and this is supported by the fact that they are all in sequence.

These circulation strikes HAD TO HAVE BEEN HANDED OUT LOCALLY because there would have been some reference to the shipment and receipt of these coins in all the letters between Patterson, Bradford and Tyler at that specific time. This is NOT an issue of lost correspondence because the letters exist in the archives. In addition, if the coins HAD BEEN SENT to Patterson, there would have been absolutely no need to produce the Smithsonian specimen later in March (along with 4 -5 others) for the Mint Cabinet collection. The quality of many of the survivors. (e.g. Eliasberg PR64, Atwater PR 63+ CAC) is more than good enough for his collection.

It has been PROVEN by John Dannreuther that there was a PROOF production run on March 27, 1839 based on the GR-1die crack on the reverse of the Smithsonian specimen, and it is PROVEN that this coin was sent to Patterson because it's been in the Mint Collection since 1839.

4-5 other proof specimens MUST have been produced at this same time and since lost because Tyler wrote that the 1838-O half dollar had a mintage "of not more than 20." Even though his letter has been lost, it's generally regarded as having been authentic. If only one 1838-O proof half dollar was struck in late March, then the total mintage would be way too low (11) versus the estimate in Tyler's letter (20), so it is logical to assume that a few more were made, sent and then lost at a later date.

It needs to be said once again that Dannreuther and Flynn have accomplished something truly exceptional in ALIGNMENT OF THE STARS! They've brought together all the historic evidence into one book, and they seem to have drawn all the right conclusions from their material.

However, there may be a few more questions that need to be asked, and these questions could mean BIG trouble in River City. You members of my treasure team have ALL the information that I have, so do YOU have any questions or see any problems? Please think about it before reading any further, after all you're part of my team and you're solving this mystery WITH me.

24

Questions for "Alignment"

DID YOU MAKE a list of questions about the conclusions in ALIGNMENT OF THE STARS ? If you did, go ahead and compare them to my list below.

1. Is it still POSSIBLE that there was a Proof run in Philadelphia before the dies were shipped to New Orleans? ALL proof coins were made in Philadelphia until 1855. There are NO exceptions other than the PROOF 1838-O and PROOF 1839-O half dollars. Mint Director Patterson often used advance production of proof coins to review design changes, and the prominent "O" mint mark right over the date was certainly a design change.

2. Is the Anderson DuPont (Cinderella Coin) really part of the same production sequence as 7 of the survivors? There are a number of important differences. It's the only specimen with no apparent die crack. It's the only specimen that seems to have the reverse marks of the catastrophic die collapse. It's the only specimen that appears to have been made under very low striking pressure. It's the only specimen that seems to have die rust on its surfaces.

3. How is it possible that the other 7 specimens from the first "circulation" run all have STRONG proof characteristics. They all

have EXTREMELY sharp detailed strikes and HIGHLY MIRRORED surfaces which is completely inconsistent with coins made for circulation that were never intended to be sent to the Mint Director.

4. How was it possible to apply such high (PROOF) strike pressure on a press when the reverse die was SPLICED in place? It 's obvious that the lowest possible striking pressure would have been used to try to avoid a collapse, which happened anyway. There was NO NEED for "proof " pressure levels in any case, because the run was to produce coins for circulation.

5. How on earth did 8 out of 10 (80%) of these circulation strikes survive at all, let alone survive in near perfect condition, if they were handed out locally in New Orleans given the environment at that time?

    Frankly, that survival rate in that condition is IMPOSSIBLE.

6. How can it be that there was only ONE survivor (20%) from the late March proof run, when the coins were shipped to Patterson, received by Patterson and stored in his Mint safe and in his cabinet collection? This survival rate is WAY too low.

7. Is it POSSIBLE that Tyler fixed the large dollar press sometime after Feb 25 and BEFORE the half dollar press became operational on March 27? If yes, he COULD have tried striking a few more 1838-O half dollars in that time period. There is no solid proof to say he did or didn't fix it.

8. WHY would the New Orleans Mint strike ANY 1838 dated half dollars on or after March 27 given the direct orders not to do so by Patterson? These direct orders were received and passed on by Bradford, and he immediately wrote Patterson that he had implemented them. There wasn't enough time for Patterson to write a second letter reversing his direct orders. He would literally have had to write both letters at the same time, and Bradford would have mentioned receiving the reversal order in his March 29 letter back to Patterson.

9. IF New Orleans DID produce some prohibited 1838-O half dollars (and we KNOW they did because of Dannreuther's research), why on earth would they send them to the very person who ordered that they never be made?

How many of these questions did you ask? Do you have others?

When Lindsey was just 3 years old, she had a VERY MOST FAVORITE stuffed animal. It was a plush, ohso soft, ohso cuddly purple and white pig. It was about the size of a watermellon, and it had a big yellow daisy on one side. To absolutely no one's surprise, she named it "purple pig." That was a bit of a mouthful for a just barely 3 year old, so she really called it "URPLE" pig, and she carried Urple pig everywhere! She carried Urple to lunch, to dinner, to bed and everywhere in between. We loved Urple too, because Urple was 100% washable. There were a few moments when Lindsey and Urple were separated, and one of those was when Urple was in the washing machine taking his weekly bath. We had to explain that he had to take his own bath because he liked a different kind of soap. It wouldn't do to have Urple bathe WITH Lindsey in the bathtub, and she already figured out that she didn't want to bathe with him in the washing machine. Sometimes Lindsey would have extremely important 3 year old business to conduct, and Urple was not invited to tag along, so she'd leave him on her bedroom floor just for a minute or two.

One day, when I was returning from a business trip to Minneapolis, I happened to pass through a number of shops in the Minneapolis airport. I was jolted out of my traveller's trance by an item for sale high up on one of the store shelves. It was another PURPLE PIG! It was absolutely identical in every single respect. It was impossible to tell the difference, except for one tiny detail. It was three times bigger! There was really no choice in the matter! I bought it then and there and smuggled it home and into our house.

Patti and I stayed in our bedroom until Lindsey was off on some of her important 3 year old business. She left her room, merrily singing to herself, and while she was gone, I made the switch. Soon, very very soon, she was right back, still singing to herself as she entered her room. The singing stopped in mid- note, and there was nothing but total silence. After about 20 seconds, she came running into our room and as she pointed behind her, she kept saying, It GROWED! It GROWED!! It GROWED!!!!

Even a three year old knows when something doesn't look right.

ALIGNMENT OF THE STARS has put all their pieces together, but it seems like some of the pieces may have been forced into place. They all seem to fit, but just like LARGE purple pig, the picture doesn't look right!

After reviewing their findings and conclusions, there's both good news and bad news.

The good news is that we now have almost all the pieces to this puzzle.

The bad news is that the solution seems to be more complicated than ever! There's compelling evidence both for and against every option. We're further away than ever from seeing how the pieces fit together, but I'll have all summer at the Cape to think about it.

25

Another Successful Dinner with Morris

WE HAD BEEN at Cape Cod all summer, and we're getting together with Morris and Laura for the first time in six months. There is A LOT to talk about!

ALIGNMENT OF THE STARS has almost all the pieces to the puzzle, but they've jammed them all together to make them fit. But they DON'T FIT, so the picture doesn't make any sense. They're missing the panther's head piece which I still have in my pocket, and I believe that one piece will rearrange all the others. Based on all the new information, it seems to me that THIS is now the most likely story of the 1838-O half dollar.

When the Philadelphia Mint hardened the 1838-O dies for use, the reverse die cracked in the process. This was not an uncommon occurrence. They used this die pair with the cracked reverse to strike 9 PROOFS for review by Mint Director Patterson, which he ALWAYS did with any significant design changes. After his approval, the 9 Proofs were put in the Mint safe which explains their high strike detail, proof mirrored surfaces and high survival rate in near perfect condition. It also explains their late appearance in the Numismatic marketplace, because they were traded out by later Mint Directors in the 1860's and 1870's rather than being available right after production in 1839.

Two sets of dies were prepared for shipment to New Orleans. One set had never been hardened, but the set with the cracked reverse had to be partially re-softened for shipment, to make it impossible to use in case of theft.

When the dies arrived in New Orleans in May 1838, they were put into storage in the hot humid New Orleans climate. In December 1838, the dies were brought out of storage for preparation for use. Tyler found that the pair that had never been hardened had rusted, while the partially hardened pair had not. He also realized that since the reverse dies were too short for the large press, he would have to "jury rig" the press to make it work. He knew this would be a very risky run, so he decided to use the rusted dies rather than the good pair, and to use lower striking pressure. Despite his precautions, the system failed after only 10 coins were struck. Nine of these original New Orleans strikes were handed out locally by Tyler and Bradford and were later lost. This theory is in line with ALIGNMENT OF THE STARS with the only difference being that a different pair of rusted dies were used in the original striking. Tyler kept the last of these "originals," because it had the damage marks that proved his story of the collapsed reverse. When Alexander Bache requested a coin, Tyler sent him the single coin he had saved.

At some point, Mint Director Patterson requested one 1838 specimen for his Mint Cabinet collection. The opening and start up of the New Orleans Branch Mint was his greatest accomplishment, so he wanted a specimen in his collection that was ACTUALLY struck in New Orleans rather than one of his Philadelphia made Proofs. This single Proof was struck on the half dollar press on the night of March 27, 1839 and then sent to Patterson.

The total number of 1838-O half dollars struck is 20 (in line with Tyler's note), and the Tyler/Bache specimen is one of only two coins that were actually made in New Orleans. The other one is the PROOF in the Smithsonian collection that was sent to Patterson.

IF MY THEORY IS RIGHT, then the Tyler Bache specimen HAS NO GR-1 DIE CRACK, AND IT DOES HAVE DIE RUST. Confirmation of these two points will prove my case. I'm feeling pretty good about this, because I can't see any die crack under a magnifying glass even after hours of study, and I'm sure the Blue green material on the coin IS die rust.

I'm not entirely sure how fascinated Morris will be with the details of my latest theory, especially since the last time I saw him, I said I was giving up my hunt. There's always been a nagging suspicion in the back of my mind that he may view my treasure hunt with a hint of amusement and more than a touch of skepticism.

We've reserved our usual table at Oakridge. I see Laura coming in first and I stand up to hug and greet her. Morris is following close behind and his limp is a whole lot worse!

"Hi Morris!" We shake hands, and I put my arm around his shoulder. "WHAT is wrong with your leg Now!"

Over the next half hour, I learn even more about how golf will always destroy you mentally and physically. Both his back and ankle got much worse over the summer, and they were such a mess that he had to go see a doctor. The doctor turned out to be an obvious "quack" with no real medical sense whatsoever! He had the audacity to SUGGEST that Morris MIGHT try giving up golf for just a short while to see if things got a little better.

"Can you even BEGIN to imagine!" Morris said. "Why does he THINK I went to see him in the first place! The whole purpose was to get some relief, so I CAN play!"

I did my best to reassure him. "What's WRONG with that doctor? Doesn't he KNOW that life isn't worth living without a golf club in your hand?"

Morris agrees that his doctor has some serious medical training deficiencies, but he's already figured out the best course of treatment on his own.

"If I just keep at it, things will work themselves out!"

"ABSOLUTELY!" I say in my most supportive tone. "Just play 36 holes every day for the next two weeks, and you'll be "fit as a fiddle!" You'll be back to your old self!"

The waiter comes by to take our orders, and Morris picks up his menu. "I know what I'M having." After we all order, he tilts his menus toward me and says "How's your treasure hunt going? Last time we talked, you said it was all over."

"No, it's not over quite YET, and I did get some encouraging news!" I tell him about my latest theory, and I end by saying;

"I really believe it's WAY more valuable than people think!" Morris is on THAT like a Bulldog!

"By PEOPLE, I assume you mean ALL the EXPERTS who have ever looked at the coin, and the people who sold it to you in the first place."

"EXACTLY!!!!" Clearly, he's beginning to see the light.

"What are you going to do now?" He asks.

"I'm going to conduct some REAL research to PROVE how valuable my coin is, and I'm going to PUBLISH a research paper that will prove it's a REAL TREASURE!"

Morris arches his right eyebrow in a look of total surprise and disbelief. Now he looks more like MR. Spock, the impossibly logical Vulcan on STAR TREK, than like Marty Lagina of OAK ISLAND, except he doesn't have pointy ears.

"Have you EVER published a research paper before?" He asks.

"Welll.........not exactly."

"Have you ever WRITTEN a research paper before?" "Not TECHNICALLY." I say, but Morris keeps pressing. He's in full bulldog mode, and he's after a bone.

"Have you EVER written ANYTHING that was PUBLISHED?"

"OF COURSE!...sort of."

"What EXACTLY have you written?" he asks.

"I'm SO glad you asked!" I respond, finally feeling back on solid ground. "I started writing some pieces last year, and I read one of them to an audience in Charleston. I handed out printed copies, AND I won an AWARD!"

"I didn't know you were a WRITER! What did you write?" His curiosity is clearly piqued.

"WELL...last year I wrote a poem for a dinner honoring the famous

Scottish poet William Topaz McGonagall.

I read it during the dinner, and it was VERY well received." I knew that saying 'William Topaz McGonagall's full name would bolster my credibility, sort of like giving me some added "provenance."

"Yes. DO go on!" Morris says, and once again there's that pesky hint of skepticism.

"Well..." I continue "It was a VERY formal affair with about 50 guests. It was "black tie," and all the MOST IMPORTANT people in Charleston were there, including several famous authors. BERNARD CORNWALL was there. Bernard has written more than 40 books, and his latest is a history of the battle of Waterloo!" I was on a roll now, so I stretched the truth just the tiniest bit. "BERNARD and I are VERY GOOD friends, and he LOVED my poem!" I' d only met Bernard twice, and I never actually heard him say WHAT he thought of my poem, but I'm sure he would have liked it.

"SO...What award did you win?" He asks.

"I was made A KNIGHT OF THE WHITE ELEPHANT OF BURMA "I say with all the pride that my new lofty title deserves.

"You were made a WHITE ELEPHANT!" Morris says incredulously.

"NO, NO! I was made a KNIGHT. It was all very properly done with a sword tapping on both shoulders while I was kneeling down and everything...AND with a REAL sword!"

In truth, I was deathly afraid my college roommate who hosted this party was going to decapitate me given the amount of wine he'd consumed, and I wasn't reassured very much when he staggered to the front dragging his sword behind him.

"I was GREATLY HONORED!"...to still be alive!...I think but don't say.

"It was VERY well received!" I repeat for emphasis just in case Morris hadn't heard me the first time.

I open my laptop to my poem and point it in Morris' direction, just to prove that I really did write something. THAT is a BIG mistake! Morris is way too fast for me. He snatches the laptop out of my hands and starts reading...first silently and then out loud. He has surprisingly fast reflexes for someone with a very bad back and a bad ankle!

"Give THAT back!"

"I will." He says "As SOON as I've finished reading your poem."
Morris starts reading out loud, but Laura and Patti don't hear anything
because they never listen to anything we say anyway,

> IN PRAISE OF THE TOASTER
> Toaster, Oh Noble toaster
> You are the humble hoaster
> of breakfasts long forgot
> With spreads of jams, of jellies and of hazelnut.
> An orgy of gizmos, brash and faddish
> for hashing both beet and radish
> have washed upon our Formica shore.
> Now they're gone and slice and dice no more!
> The microwave, the blender and the roaster
> still cling to counter space.
> But none can touch our faithful toaster,
> who never loafs or toasts in haste!
> Years before we all were born
> and years aft' we all are dead
> the noble toaster stands immortal,
> without whom Toast would just be Bread.
> TO A KING, AMONG THE GIANTS
> OF ALL OUR COUNTER SPACE,
> LET US RAISE OUR GLASS AND DRAIN IT BARE
> IN A TOAST TO TOASTERS EVERYWHERE!

Morris has a very odd look on his face.

"You got an award for THIS!" He says in total disbelief.

"YES , YES INDEED! It was VERY well received" I say for the third
time, hoping it will finally stick.

"HOW MUCH did they have to drink?" He asks.

"A tiny bit...hardly enough to be worth mentioning. After all, it WAS a celebration of the famous Scottish poet WILLIAM TOPAZ McGONAGALL."

"I'll BET!" Morris exclaims, and then he starts typing on my laptop.

"STOP! WHAT ARE YOU DOING?"

"I'm JUST checking out this famous McGonagall guy. I've never heard of him!"

He finds the Wikipedia website and starts reading.

"GIVE THAT BACK!"

"NOT YET! I'm still reading." And then he begins reading out loud again.

"William Topaz McGonagall is widely regarded as the WORST poet who ever lived. In many places around the world, formal dinners are held where his poems are read and guests are encouraged to read their own dreadful creations."

Morris has an amused smirk on his face. The bulldog has apparently found his bone, and he's never going to let it go!

"SO, you got an award for the AWFULNESS of your writing?"

I HAVE to respond

"It takes INCREDIBLE talent to write truly awful poetry. Not everyone can do it! AND, I'll bring ALL this talent to bear when I write my research paper." I counter defensively, and then I add...

"I've written some other poems that are EVEN BETTER ! Do you want to see them?"

"NO!" Morris doesn't say "No thank you" or "Not right now" or "Maybe later." He just says "NO!"

If I had been a more sensitive person, my feelings might have been hurt, but I'm on a mission, and I'll remain undaunted by any skeptics.

"SO, exactly HOW will your poetic genius help in writing your research paper?" He asks.

Finally, THAT was an easy one. Now Morris was just being dense.

"Everyone knows that research papers are dull and boring. They should be used in hospitals as an anesthetic!

By adding my poetic color and flair, people will read more than just the first two lines.

MY paper will be a JOY to read, AND everyone will remember it!"

I feel certain I won both the discussion and the entire evening through clear overpowering logic, so it was another successful Monday night dinner with Morris.

26

The Research Plan

AFTER MY DINNER with Morris, I decide it's time to get moving on my research plan. A couple of things are clear. I absolutely HAVE to answer the questions raised in ALIGNMENT OF THE STARS about the ANDERSON DUPONT specimen. The authors are two of the most respected experts in American Numismatics, and I need equally respected experts to study my coin. Those experts would be the coin grading company NGC. I already have their agreement that they'll relabel the coin "EX TYLER/ BACHE" when they put it in their new holder. They would have to open the old holder anyway, so this would be the best time to have them do an exhaustive study of the coin outside of its holder. ALIGNMENT wrote that the only way to resolve the question of dirt on the coin and the reverse marks would be conduct an out of holder examination, so we'll DO IT!

I need NGC to definitively answer the following questions:

1. Does the reverse have a GR-1 die crack?
   If yes, how developed is it compared to other specimens, and is it worn away?
2. Are the marks on the lower reverse real or just "dirt?"
3. Is the blue green substance on the surface of the coin just circulation dirt?

IF it's just dirt, IT WILL BE EASY TO REMOVE A SAMPLE for chemical analysis.

IF it isn't dirt, then it will be part of the coin and IT WON'T BE POSSIBLE TO REMOVE A SAMPLE.

4. Take the highest possible resolution photographs for a permanent record while the coin is out of its holder.
5. Re holder the coin and relabel it as "EX TYLER/ BACHE."

I'll get NGC's agreement to this plan in the next two months before Christmas, and assuming they agree, I'll send the coin off to them in early January. FINALLY, the "ANDERSON DUPONT" name will be gone, and its true provenance will be reflected in its new name forever. If nothing else happens, that alone will be a GREAT achievement!

By January 10, 2016 I've made all the arrangements with NGC, and they've agreed to the research plan and, once again, to the name change on the holder label. It was time to send the coin off. Now this isn't quite as easy as you might think. After all, it was sent to me in an ARMORED car. NGC is located in Sarasota, Florida, and sending an armored car from Savannah to Sarasota is WAY out of my budget. I went to the U.S. Post office and learned that Insurance over $100,000 is also a special deal and hugely expensive. I've never had a package lost by the Post Office, so I boxed up the coin, wrapped it, taped it, boxed it again and then sealed the whole thing with duct tape. I insured it for $50,000 and sent it off in a US Post Office box to NGC. I was a nervous wreck until I got a call three days later from NGC that my package was safely in their hands. They'll need a blowtorch to open it, but that's their problem now!

I'm 95% sure what their research results will show, so now it's just a question of waiting, and the waiting will take some time ! After NGC removes the coin from its old holder, they'll take the highest resolution digital photographs possible of the obverse, the reverse and the edge. They'll send me copies of these images as soon as they're done.

Next, the coin will be carefully examined and studied by at least three of their top Numismatic experts. After that, they'll attempt to remove a tiny sample of the "dirt" for chemical and/or spectrographic analysis. Finally, it will be placed in a new holder, relabeled and sent back to me. This whole process will take more than two months!

The first step doesn't take long! On January 20, there's an email from NGC with three files containing the 3 images.

I have butterflies in my stomach as I click on the first file. These images will tell the story! Depending on what they show it could be "game over" and the end of my treasure hunt, or it could confirm my theory. The first file opens and I'm stunned!

The picture is far sharper and brighter than I ever dared hope! The lighting has actually penetrated the black toning, and there are many hints of uncirculated gold coming through around the edges. This PROVES my contention that the black discoloration is due to extreme toning. Most importantly, the blue green debris is EVERYWHERE. It's around the edges of every feature...the hair, the date, the bust. The blue green color is now MUCH brighter and easier to see. This is clearly NOT circulation dirt. It HAS to be the Iron Hydroxide that forms when steel rusts! There is no longer any doubt, but the PROOF will come when NGC tries to remove a sample. Any kind of circulation debris can be easily removed, BUT if it is die rust. It will be impossible to remove because it will be part of the coin.

I click on the second file which has the image of the reverse. It's every bit as good as the first, but this image is the most important. It will tell me if the reverse marks are real and if there is a GR-1 die crack. I enlarge this image as much as possible, and I don't see any die crack. The reverse marks are clearer than ever and it's easy to see how the metal from the coin itself has been "plowed" by the raised dentils on the reverse die when it collapsed. Each dentil acted as a tiny snow plow leaving a miniature pile of scraped metal from the coin at the end of each furrow. These images are VERY GOOD NEWS!

They support my theory that a different pair of rusted dies were used to strike the coin in New Orleans, and THAT would mean that the others were made as PROOFS in Philadelphia. This is SUCH good news that I decide I can write my research report with all my conclusions NOW and just fill in the research result specifics when they're officially published by NGC. This will save a lot of time! Despite what I told Morris about applying my poetic genius to make a research report that is "a joy to read," I decide that I'll bury my readers in evidence and facts instead.

By March 1 my research paper is done! It's 19 pages long and has all the supporting archival letters along with my internet research on steel rust, the sulfur content of early 19th century paper and the chemical interaction that causes toning. It even includes a section on the Mathematics and Physics that prove the reverse marks had to have been caused by the collapsed reverse die. All I need now is to insert NGC's research findings and I can send it off for publication.

When I was 12, I had a friend named Michael. Michael lived in the city of Worcester and I lived in the country outside the city. Occasionally, I would go to his house on a Saturday to spend the day. When you live in the country, there's always a ton of stuff to do with lots of exciting adventures if you just use your imagination.. All of these adventures were OUTSIDE, exploring the woods , following rivers and even getting lost in cornfields when the stalks are high enough. INSIDE was NOT fun and gets boring very quickly!

So I was at Michael's house, and we were inside all day or, at best, outside in his very small back yard. We weren't allowed to just go wandering around the city by ourselves because we MIGHT get in trouble. We weren't REALLY the trouble seeking kind of kids and maybe it would've been best if Michael's mother had just let us go. But she was going to be gone all afternoon, so what would happen if we DID get in trouble in the city. "NO!" she said "You boys will just have to stay home so you don't get in any trouble!"

It got boring VERY quickly. You go a hundred feet in any direction in the city and you end up in someone else's living room. We went up to Michael's bed room where there's even more nothing whatsoever to do. All of a sudden, that changed in an instant!

"What's THAT?" I said. "I've never noticed THAT before!"

I was pointing to a very large glass jar on the top of his bureau.

"There's stuff in it ! What's in it?" I asked with a growing curiosity.

"Oh...nothing. Just a bunch of old match books my parents collected from every place they ever visited. They saved 'em and put 'em in that jar sort of like a display 'cause you

can see the names of all the different places they've been."
Michael answered with less than no enthusiasm.

"There must be THOUSANDS!"

"Who cares where they've been?" he yawned.

Now Michael is a good guy, but he has absolutely NO
sense of adventure and not a very big pile of imagination
either.

"DO YOU HAVE A TENNIS BALL CAN?" I asked hopefully.

"Yes, but the tennis courts are a mile from here and we're
NOT suppose to leave the house. We might get in trouble."

See what I mean. NO IMAGINATION whatsoever!

"Michael, can you find the tennis ball can? I have an idea
that MIGHT be interesting."

He went out to the garage and came back with an old
yellow tennis ball can filled with a bunch of old balls. The
day was starting to look a little better and might not be so
boring after all ! I dumped the balls out on the floor and they
bounced around before rolling under his bed. Have you ever
noticed that every time you dump a can of tennis balls on the
floor, they ALWAYS roll someplace where it's impossible to
get them? NO MATTER. I wasn't interested in the tennis balls
anyway.

"Michael, do you think you can find a couple of pairs of
scissors?"

Two minutes later he was back with the scissors.

Just in case it isn't 100 % clear where I was going with
this, it's worth pointing out that Worcester was the home of
Dr Robert Goddard who is the father of modern rocketry and
everybody knows THAT! Now, I'm NOT dumb! I know that
"children should NEVER play with matches," but that obviously didn't apply here. This situation is COMPLETELY different.
First, I'm TWELVE years old! That's just one year short of being a teenager, which is right next to being an adult. Second,
I'd never dream of PLAYING with matches! NO! That would

be SO wrong! I was going to EXPERIMENT with matches. THIS would be real scientific research...maybe even breakthrough research!

We had all the raw material for experimentation, so the only thing left to do was to decide on a worthy experiment and then do the engineering. We both agreed that building a rocket was a most worthy experiment , so we set about cutting all the heads off the match sticks. Michael was in charge of solid fuel development, so he did all the cutting.

"There goes the Bermuda Beach club!" He noted.

"Couldn't go to a better cause!" I answered.

I was in charge of loading the solid fuel, and I was also "lift off" specialist because it was my idea in the first place.

I dumped piles of match heads into the can.

"TOO LOOSE! WAY TOO LOOSE!" I announced from mission control in a panicky voice. "We need to CRAM them in so they're packed as tight as possible! Otherwise we may not achieve low earth orbit."

Michael stopped cutting and went downstairs. He returned with his mother's 17th century antique mortar and pestle.

"PERFECT!" I exclaiming as I began pounding the mass of match heads into a solid mass inside the can.

"More match heads! We need MORE match heads! Our launch window is closing!"

It was impossible to put any more match heads into the can and Michael's room was littered with scraps of cardboard matchbook covers and headless matchsticks. It looked like Times Square an hour after New year's.

Michael said "Don't forget to SAVE one for lift off."

THAT was a most excellent point! In all the enthusiasm of loading rocket fuel, I'd forgotten about lift off, and we'd pretty much cleaned his house out of matches.

"I'll save TWO, just in case there's an ignition failure on the first try!"

I'd crammed at least 5000 match heads into the can, so one less shouldn't make too much of a difference.

It was LAUNCH TIME, and as launch specialist I decided the launch should take place in the back yard for a bunch of very good reasons. First, launching in Michael's bedroom was obviously out of the question, because our rocket would NEVER reach our target of low Earth orbit. We both under-stood that the ceiling was in the way. Second, there were spies EVERYWHERE, and the back yard was the most secure outside location. We could conduct our experiment away from prying eyes. Besides, we were told not to leave the back yard. We went out to the back yard to build our launch pad. I set three small flat rocks on the ground.

"Why the rocks?" Michael asked

"I'm sure not going to HOLD it when we set this thing off! Do YOU want to hold it?" Common sense! THIS was why I was launch specialist. I carefully set the fully loaded can on the three flat rocks as if it was a bomb, and then I adjusted it right and left until it was perfectly upright.

"We don't want it to go off SIDEWAYS, because we won't get much altitude if it goes sideways." I said knowingly.

"We won't get much altitude it it doesn't go up at all!" Michael added. I ignored his comment, because I had abso-lute confidence in the project, and I sensed he was starting to have some reservations at the most critical moment.

I'd left a good space underneath the rocket platform to light the matches and for air to fuel the fire.

It was Time! 10...9...8...7...6...5...4...3!...2!...1! "IGNITION!" I lit the match and held it under the can until the match heads started to catch. The flames started to shoot out of the bot-tom from between the rocks. They got bigger and bigger, and then the can started to rise from its platform.

"WE HAVE LIFTOFF!" I shouted loud enough for every spy within two miles to hear. The rocket continued to rise, very slowly at first, but then it started to gain speed. An inch, two inches, then 5 and then 5 feet and 10 feet. It kept going straight up, faster and faster. It was a totally MAGNIFICENT sight as it soared into the sky! Except then I noticed something a bit odd.

"I thought our can was YELLOW." I said to Michael. Michael agreed that it was indeed yellow and all of his mother's tennis ball cans in his garage were yellow.

"Then WHY is it ORANGE?"

"It SHOULDN'T be orange. It should be yellow like the rest of the cans." He looked up and squinted. Our rocket was now more than 100 feet up.

"It ISN'T Orange." he said.

"Thank goodness!" I thought for a moment that the blinding light from the liftoff had damaged my eyes.

"It's BRIGHT RED!" Michael added.

Our rocket was now more than 200 feet in the air.

"It shouldn't be RED and it shouldn't be ORANGE either! It's suppose to be YELLOW!"

While we were arguing about the color, it ran out of fuel and started to come down.

"OH-OH! WE HAVE INCOMING! WE'RE UNDER ATTACK! RUN!"

I shouted, just in case all the neighborhood spies were asleep.

"RUN WHERE?" Michael asked, pointing at the high wooden fence that surrounded his very small back yard.

"RUN ANYWHERE! RUN EVERYWHERE!

JUST RUN!" I yelled, just in case the neighborhood spies were STILL asleep.

Unfortunately, this is where the planning part of our experiment ended. We hadn't thought about reentry at all, because it isn't an immediate issue once you've achieved low Earth orbit.

Our rocket came ALMOST straight down and it glowed redder and redder as it fell. I say "ALMOST" straight down, because if it had come EXACTLY straight down, it would've landed right back on its landing pad instead of on Michael's roof.

As soon as it hit the roof, the bright red can stuck right into the asphalt shingles. It didn't bounce, and smoke started curling up from the shingles and THAT was quickly followed by flames, and a plume of black smoke started to rise from the roof, clearly visible to all the neighborhood spies.

We were very lucky. There was an upstairs dormer window near our rocket's final resting place. We both grabbed buckets , filled them with water, and raced upstairs. Fortunately asphalt shingles don't burn quite as fast as wooden ones, but they sure do make a lot of smoke! After we put the fire out, Michael was worried that his mother might find out, and I tried to reassure him.

"Your mother almost never climbs out THAT upstairs window to go out on the roof, and even IF she did, AND she saw the burn marks, you can just tell her it must have been a lightning strike."

I also pointed out that our rocket landing was MUCH BETTER than any rocket landings the Government had done recently.

"Another 4 feet to the left , and BULLSEYE! It would have gone right down the chimney!"

When you do a research experiment, you can never know for certain what the results will be. On March 10, I receive a call from NGC. They have the results from my study.

27

A Torpedo Through the Midsection of Our Treasure Hunt

THE PHONE RINGS, and I pick it up without much thought . I hadn't expected a call from NGC. I thought they'd send me a written report.

"Hi...this is Tom from NGC. Is this Kin?"

"Yes! Hi Tom. What have you got?" I answer more than a little bit nervously. I feel like I'm back in college and about to get my grade on a final exam.

"I thought I'd give you a call before we reholdered your coin, just in case there was something more you wanted us to do. We spent a lot of time carefully examining it, and here are the top line results from our evaluation. First, it HAS the GR-1 die crack. It's in a VERY early state, but it can be seen between the "H" and the "A" in "HALF DOLLAR" on the bottom reverse. There's NO wear that has reduced the extent, the visibility or appearance of the crack."

I'm absolutely SHOCKED by this conclusion. I'd spent HOURS looking for the crack and never saw the slightest indication of one!

"Are you 100% SURE? I studied the images you sent in January, and I couldn't see any crack."

I try not to show disappointment in my voice.

"We ARE 100% certain the crack IS there. We had three of our best experts study it, and they ALL agree. It's in a VERY minimal state, so it's VERY hard to see, but it IS definitely there." Tom said, and then he continued with NGC's assessment.

"Regarding the marks on the lower reverse, they ARE real. We physically probed them. They're PART of the coin and not any kind of dirt or debris. There's no question about that."

At least THAT was true.

"What about the blue green residue all over the surfaces? Were you able to get a sample?" I asked.

"THAT is most unusual." Tom replies. "We TRIED several times to remove some, but we had no luck. We finally stopped, because we were afraid we might DAMAGE the coin. That blue green material is either PART of the coin or it's FUSED to the coin, so It ISN'T dirt from circulation! It's strange. We don't believe it's die rust either, because the pattern is WRONG. The pattern seems to be the same as if dust had been blown across the coin surfaces so it ended up in all the cracks and crevasses of the impression. It's NOT what we'd expect to see with die rust."

"Tom, I REALLY need you to try again to get a sample. Chemically that stuff has all the characteristics of STEEL DIE RUST, but I can't PROVE it without a sample to test. The sample can be really small... TINY! I don't need much, and maybe you can get it from close to the edge where it won't show."

"We'll give it another try." Tom said. I thank him and we hang up.

This is truly AWFUL news! The GR-1 die crack IS there! I don't believe it! If the crack is there, then our treasure hunt is OVER. Since ALL the 1838-O specimens have the crack, then they all HAD to be made from the SAME pair of dies. Since the crack is minimal, my coin was struck before the others AND struck in New Orleans per Tyler's own written words. That means they ALL were struck in New Orleans! The ONLY REASON my coin might be an extremely valuable undiscovered treasure is if it was the ONLY ONE (or the only one excluding the Smithsonian specimen) that was made in New Orleans. Then my coin would be one of only two legitimate 1838-O half dollars and potentially worth a fortune. True, we've established its history and provenance all the way back to 1839, and that's no small thing, but this "Torpedo" report from NGC has blown my theory AND my pre-written research paper sky high!

I STILL don't believe it! I'll send NGC's high resolution image and their assessment to Dave Stone at Heritage to see what he thinks.

It doesn't take long! Dave sends my NGC image back, with a thin red line penciled in marking where he THINKS he sees the die crack between the "H" and the "A." He says he's sure it's there, because it seems to have the same location and shape as the much more developed cracks on other 1838-O's.

It really IS over, but there's one more thing I want to do. I call up the Photographer at NGC who took the pictures and ask him to take ONE more before the coin goes into its new holder. I ask him to use the highest possible resolution and to focus in on just the "H" and the "A," where the crack is visible. In addition, I ask him to adjust his lighting angle to maximize the crack. This is the mistake ALIGNMENT made when they looked at an image of the ATWATER specimen, because the lighting angle didn't show the die crack.

In the next two weeks I get my additional questions answered by NGC.

The new high resolution image comes in, and I HAVE to agree! The die crack IS there! It's barely visible, but it has exactly the same jagged shape between the "H" and the "A" as the cracks on all the others.

Tom calls me and tells me that they tried again to get a sample of the blue green material, but they couldn't do it without damage. I thank him and ask him to re label and re holder the coin, and send it back to me.

This whole thing confuses me now more than ever! Given these results, Is it still POSSIBLE that the proofs were struck in Philadelphia? Could they have repaired the cracked die before sending it to New Orleans? That's the only way I could explain why the GR-1 crack on my coin would be smaller and less developed than those on coins that were produced EARLIER in Philadelphia.

Now, I'm beginning to sound just like the people on the TV show "ANCIENT ALIENS." "Is it POSSIBLE that ancient aliens came to Earth to harvest SKUNK CABBAGE? SOME Ancient Astronaut theorists THINK SO!"

I write several experts on early coin dies, and it turns out that it ISN'T POSSIBLE! Reheating, softening and then re-hardening the dies only makes the crack worse. Die cracks ARE NOT repairable, and ancient aliens didn't come to Earth to harvest skunk cabbage.

In the fall of 1959, my brother David had just started his Freshman year at Yale University. It was Parent's Weekend, and my mother and father had made the trip to New Haven to see him. The first year students lived on what was called "The Old Campus," which was located right in the center of New Haven. This was a huge quadrangle building with a park dotted with ancient oak trees in the center. All the rooms were in the tall building that completely surrounded the central park, and the only way in was through one of four large Iron Gates, one on each side of the quadrangle.

My parents walked though the main gate at about 9am on Saturday morning and wandered around for a good 10 minutes looking for David's room. They knew they were in the right General area, but all the towers and entry ways looked the same.

Finally, in frustration my father looked up, and he saw two boys leaning out of a third story window. He called up to them.

"DOES DAVID CARMODY LIVE HERE?"
One of the boys answered back.
"JUST LEAVE HIM ON THE DOORSTEP!"

Sometimes when you ask a question, you get the answer to a question you DID NOT ask.

I had sent my coin to NGC to prove that it was the only one actually minted in New Orleans. The answer I got back was that ALL the 1838-O's were made in New Orleans, but they also answered a question I didn't ask." Where does my coin fit in the sequence of production?" The answer to THAT question WAS answered. Since it has the least developed GR-1 die crack, that PROVES it's the FIRST PRODUCED 1838-O half dollar of all the known survivors. That's one more piece to the puzzle, AND being FIRST is a real plus! I learned that from my comic book fiasco. Being FIRST isn't even in the same ballpark with being the ONLY ONE made in New Orleans, but I CAN say it's the earliest known half dollar ever produced at any branch mint. Now THAT makes my coin HISTORICALLY IMPORTANT! My Treasure hunt has uncovered the most complete "Provenance" possible going all the way back to the Coiner who produced it in 1839, AND it has proven its historical importance. These two things will add some value, so this whole project hasn't been a complete failure!

We COULD stop now, but I don't think so! My theory about the 1838-O half dollars isn't right, but neither is the one in ALIGNMENT OF THE STARS. NOW, we have more pieces to this puzzle than they have, so I'm going to keep on searching until we get the final answer. I still believe that my CINDERELLA COIN is the key to solving the mystery, just like the PANTHER HEAD with its golden eyes.

For nearly a thousand years, sailors have seen SEA SERPENTS, and their descriptions are often the same.

These serpents are like giant snakes with spines running down their backs, and they appear to be at least 100 feet long!

Witnesses have described huge snake coils looping in the ocean, and then the serpent will take off in one direction before diving out of sight. Most people think this must be pure fantasy, but many old maps have these very same pictures of sea serpents decorating their oceans and borders. In 1900, more than 150 people watched from the shores of

Marblehead, Massachusetts as a sea serpent frolicked in the ocean for at least 20 minutes, and this account was published in Newspapers all across the U.S. We're they ALL delusional?

It was mid July 2012, and I was sitting in our sunroom in Cape Cod reading a paper. Our sunroom looks out over Nauset Beach and the ocean beyond, and it was a beautiful day with bright blue sky and no clouds. About a quarter of a mile out was a SEA SERPENT that was AT LEAST 100 feet long. I had my binoculars, so I was able to watch it closely for about 15 seconds. It swam left to right, writhing as it moved, and its coils and back fins were clearly visible as it moved through the waves.Then it went under, never to resurface again!

My account was written up in all the local papers in Cape Cod, not because I'd seen a sea serpent , but because for the first time in 1000 years someone knew what it really was! This is what REALLY happened.

I was looking out at the ocean, when I saw a huge commotion with enormous splashes of water about a quarter of a mile out. I picked up my binoculars to see what was going on. I adjusted the focus, and it came into view. It was a pod of about 10 Minke Whales in total turmoil. Suddenly they all went under and resurfaced, forming a perfect chain. I couldn't see any heads or tails, and their bodies were so closely joined, they looked like a linked chain of loops. Each Minke Whale has a dorsal fin, so the effect was a row of spines running down the back of a single snake-like creature. After it went under, I realized that these sea serpents sightings have ALWAYS been pods of whales, because snakes CAN'T swim through water that way. Their coils have to move side to side for traction, not UP and DOWN. Only animals with fluked tails could could move like that !

We see what we expect to see, and we see what we want to see. Our minds will fill in the missing pieces to make the picture work.

ALIGNMENT OF THE STARS may have forced its evidence into a picture that they already believed.

Then, I turned around and did EXACTLY the same thing. I was so wedded to he idea that most of the other specimens were made in Philadelphia, that I tried to make the evidence fit MY picture.

IF we're going to solve this thing, we have to let the facts dictate the solution, not the other way around. We have to look at all the puzzle pieces, fit them together easily and naturally without force, and only then will we be able to see the whole picture as it really is.

28

Schrödinger Returns

I **HAD HOPED** to call my coin "THE CINDERELLA COIN," because I believed that this tarnished and "dirty" specimen was in reality something very special! I had hoped that a professional research study of the coin would reveal its true identity just like Cinderella. While the NGC report does show that the coin is the first branch Mint half dollar ever made, the others were made right after, so it doesn't support the "Cinderella" name. From now on, it will have be known as "THE TYLER BACHE" specimen which reflects its unequalled history and lineage, and that's now the name on its holder.

One week later, I receive the coin in the mail. This time it's the U.S. postman who delivers it. I have to sign, but NO ARMORED CAR and no opportunity to excite all the criminals in the neighborhood, who are probably still skulking around my house. I open the box, and there it is! MY COIN IS IN A HOLDER THAT SAYS "EX TYLER BACHE!" Its old ANDERSON DUPONT name is gone forever! I bask in this one piece of success for a full two minutes, but then a sense of panic starts to set in. I grab my safe deposit key and rush to the bank to get it back in its box where it belongs. As I put it back in the box, it reminds me of my poor imaginary cat, SCHRÖDINGER, when he was put in HIS box.

NOW, it's time for us to put the pieces together and finally solve this puzzle! All the pieces seem to swirl around my head, and they don't fit together, and they don't make any sense.

All the other coins have sharp, high pressure strikes and mirrored proof surfaces, while TYLER/BACHE seems to have been struck under much lower pressure and doesn't seem to have these same surfaces. How could coins with such sharp high pressure strikes have been made on dies that were spliced together and couldn't withstand high pressures?

All nine coins have the GR-1 die crack, so they were all made from the same dies.

Tyler Bache seems to have steel die rust, but the pattern of that rust is unusual.

None of the other coins have any of this blue green material. Is this something that happened after the coin was struck? If that's true, it should've been easy to remove a sample, but NGC believes it's part of the coin.

Why is Tyler Bache the only specimen that shows any marks from the collapsing of the reverse die support?

How did the other 8 specimens survive in such a hostile environment for 180 years in near perfect condition?

Why would the New Orleans Mint strike ANY 1838-O half dollars at all, after having been directly ordered not to do so by The Director of the U.S. Mint? The Superintendent of the New Orleans Mint confirmed his order and passed it on to his Chief Coiner.

Why would the New Orleans Mint then send these banned coins to the very same person who ordered them never be made?

It's simply NOT POSSIBLE that the Mint Director could have sent another letter reversing his earlier order and requesting that the Proofs be made, and that his letter countermanding that order has been lost. Patterson's order would have been received on about March 25, so there wouldn't have been time to write another letter before the Smithsonian sample was made on, or just shortly after, the night of March 27. Even IF there were such a letter, Superintendent Bradford would HAVE to have mentioned it in the letter he wrote to Patterson on March 29 to tell him that they'd made his newly requested coin.

WHY is there absolutely NO written record of a second production, even though it's been PROVEN that it took place and at least one coin was produced? There should be SOME letter somewhere that mentions the making, shipping or receiving of this coin. There are a couple of letters that document the original January 1839 run, but nothing on this one. Why not?

Why would the New Orleans Mint make ANY proof half dollars ? There's absolutely no reason they should make any PROOFS, because those kinds of coins were entirely the province of the Philadelphia mint. YET, it's been PROVEN that they struck at least one 1838, and as many as four 1839 PROOFS at the same time, and all these coins have been classified as Proofs for more than 100 years. We have no evidence that anyone ever requested any of these proofs, and it was an action that was never repeated at any Branch Mint until 1855, when a few were made to commemorate the opening of the New San Francisco Mint.

How can we account for a total mintage of "not more than twenty" which was written by Tyler in his note wrapped around the Tyler Bache specimen? ALIGNMENT OF THE STARS had to fudge their own theory to get to the number up to15, which they felt was "in the ballpark" of 20. Fifteen is still too low, because Tyler wrote "not more than 20" in his note. Since HE'S the one who made all the coins in New Orleans, he should know! However, he wouldn't know the exact number, if some had been produced in Philadelphia.

All current Numismatic guide books have recognized the mintage number of 20 for the past hundred years. Are they all wrong?

All these pieces keep swirling around my head...around and around! None ever come together, and none ever fit. We CAN'T make the same mistake and try to force these pieces into a theory. We HAVE to fit the pieces together first, and ONLY THEN can we see the final picture. It's very disappointing, because I've been at it for weeks and it's not coming together. Part of the problem is that I keep trying to get the pieces to fit together all at once into a new theory, and that's WRONG! We HAVE to do this the exact same way I do a puzzle...just fit one piece at a time.

That night I go to bed and have a restless night with a lot of tossing, turning and rolling over, and a lot of Patti asking "WHAT'S wrong?" When she asks that, she really means "What's wrong with YOU? Why are you acting this way?"

Finally, I fall into a fitful sleep and have another one of my weird dreams.

I'm sitting at a table, and there are jigsaw puzzle pieces in a pile in the middle. The pieces are all different colors and there aren't any flat edge pieces at all, so none have been connected. It's just a pile in the middle. I don't touch any of them. I just sit staring at them! My mood darkens, as storm clouds of frustration start to gather, and the winds of disappointment begin to blow. At first it's just a breeze, but soon it becomes a howling gale outside my door bringing with it a downpour of despair!

Then, there's a barely audible scratching somewhere at the back of my mind. It gets louder, and I realize the scratching is coming from outside. Something is trying to get in! At first It's barely audible, but it gets louder and louder and more persistent. I get up from the table and open the door. There is SCHRÖDINGER! He's bedraggled and half drowned, but he's there! He wants IN, and wants in NOW!

"What are YOU doing here? I thought you were dead!"

Schrödinger ambles into the room, as if he owns the place and meouls loudly. He seems to be somewhat annoyed with my damp mood, but at least HE'S dry now.

The storm outside is gone and the puzzle and table have vanished too. Schrödinger wants to be picked up and petted, so I do. He tilts his head so I can rub him under his chin and behind his ears.

He starts purring, and I wake up.

The next morning, all the puzzle pieces are still swirling around my head like a swarm of angry bees, and I think of my dream. All of a sudden it hits me like a thunderbolt. Schrödinger has the answer! SCHRÖDINGER IS THE ANSWER! There are two totally incompatible and opposite states existing at the same time...IN THE CINDERELLA COIN! The Cinderella coin is just like Schrödinger's cat. I've always said that every object has two stories to tell. One story is how it came to be, and the other is the impact of everything that's ever touched it. The story is ALWAYS there. You just have to see it and know how to read it.

Just as quickly, two pieces click together and fall on my imaginary table. Then two more, and then with a rush, ALL THE PIECES FALL, and they're all locked together in place. I look down, and for the very first time I can see the complete picture and the solution to this 180 year old mystery. Even better, it isn't just a THEORY. It's absolute and un-equivocal PROOF, and it's been right in front of me all the time!

29

How to Make a Presentation with Teeth

IT SOUNDS LIKE a riddle. "Why is the CINDERELLA COIN like Schrödinger's cat?"

The answer is: "Because they both occupy impossible opposite and incompatible states at the same time."

In quantum physics, Schrödinger's cat is BOTH dead and alive until his box is opened. These are impossible opposite and incompatible states.

The Cinderella coin is BOTH the first AND the last coin struck in the January 1839 original circulation run. It has the least developed GR-1 die crack, so it's the first. It's the only specimen that has the marks of the collapsed reverse, so it has to be the last. Any coin struck after CINDERELLA MUST have even more severe reverse die marks, but none of the others has even the slightest indication of the collapsed reverse die. The reverse die marks on CINDERELLA LINE UP PERFECTLY with the GR -1 crack on the die, so now we know that the collapse of the reverse is the event that cracked the die. Since the Schrödinger's cat analogy just applies to quantum physics, the only way CINDERELLA can be both first and last at the same time, is if it's THE ONLY SURVIVOR from this first production run. This is now more than just a theory. These two pieces of physical evidence absolutely PROVE it's the only surviving original circulation strike.

With this piece of the puzzle PROVEN, all the other pieces start to fall into place.

Since CINDERELLA is first, then NONE of the surviving 1838-O half dollars could have been struck EARLIER in Philadelphia. THIS IS NOW PROVEN!

Since CINDERELLA is last, then all the other specimens were struck on the half dollars press on the night of March 27, when it became operational. It's still REMOTELY possible that Tyler repaired the large dollar press and struck a few 1838 half dollars before March 27, but this is extremely unlikely. Fixing the large press and attempting another run would have required some mention in the archival letters we have for that time period, and there is no such mention. In addition, John Dannreuther has already PROVEN that at least one PROOF (The Smithsonian specimen) WAS STRUCK on that night, and he speculates that as many as five were made. It's now logical to believe that all 10 were made in that second run, which adds up to a total of 20, consistent with Tyler's note.

We can now state (if not absolutely prove) that all the other eight survivors were struck AS PROOFS on the night of March 27 and were later sent to Mint Director Patterson. This explains both their superb quality and their high strike pressure details. The CINDERELLA COIN was struck under low pressure and shows weak strike details, but since it's unique, it's the only one with this characteristic.

Finally, the "die rust" piece falls into place. We know from the gouge marks on its reverse, that the reverse die had some horizontal motion when it collapsed. This would have resulted in steel on steel abrasion producing steel "dust" in the process. This steel dust was imbedded into the coin in striking, and then rusted in place in the years while it was wrapped in Tyler's note. The blue green residue is in fact DIE STEEL RUST on the coin, but the coin itself was not struck from rusted dies.

At this point, all the pieces of this puzzle are in place as to WHAT HAPPENED AND WHEN.

"WHY" as many as 10 PROOFS were struck on the night of March 27, contrary to the Mint Director's highly specific written orders, has not yet been answered. We can't write a solid research report that solves the 1838-O mystery until we have a compelling answer to this question, so there's still more work to be done.

Now, it's clear that CINDERELLA is A REAL PRINCESS ! She is the only survivor from the first circulation run, while all the others are PROOF RESTRIKES. THAT means the CINDERELLA COIN is THE ONLY SURVIVING CIRCULATION STRIKE 1838-O HALF DOLLAR, and THAT'S a big deal! It also means that it's the rarest U.S. coin ever made for circulation, because it's UNIQUE, and because it was the SHORTEST CIRCULATION RUN EVER MADE (only 10 coins).

It's time to rewrite my research report, while I try to figure out WHY these things were done. My NEW Research report can't have any holes. It's got to be PROOF, NOT JUST A THEORY, and it can't be boring. It has to have TEETH !

About ten years ago, our Nauset beach community on Cape Cod decided it would be endless fun to have a sand castle/ sand sculpture contest JUST for people who lived in Nauset Hights. Anyone could enter as long as they were from Nauset Heights, and that included adults, children of any age and even entire families with outside guests. There would be judging by local artists and small trophies handed out to the winners in whatever categories those judges decided should be represented. In their infinite wisdom, the judges always decided what the categories should be AFTER they saw all the sand sculptures. THAT WAY, they could create categories for any worthy entry they felt should win. Best of all, there were NO professional sand sculptors involved, so everyone had a chance to win, ESPECIALLY the kids. After all, that's what this whole contest was about.

The first year, my friend Bob entered with his family, and he won the top prize, "BEST ON THE BEACH," for his sand sculpture of a VW Beetle. It was really good, with a sand windshield and sand tires and everything!That was the last time Bob entered. I asked him why, and he told me that a VW was the only thing he could ever make out of sand that looked like anything. He'd been doing the exact same VW on Nauset Beach every year for the past 30 years for his kids. Having won the very first contest, he thought it best to retire, so he could "go out on top." The next year, Bob's daughter, Susan, entered to try and extend their family winning streak of one, but she had two fatal strikes against her. First, she was forty years old and the Judges really wanted a kid to win. Second, and maybe most important, her sculpture was of the Museum of Modern Art. She thought that would appeal to the artistic inclination of the judges, and she'd be a sure winner. Unfortunately, no one on the beach that day had the slightest idea what she'd made. I was pretty sure it was suppose to be building of some kind, and I congratulated her on her most excellent reproduction of the Boston Bus Station. Susan wasn't pleased with my misidentification, and let me know immediately that I was obviously a cultural boor and must have dropped out of school before third grade. THAT'S when I decided to throw my hat into the sand sculpture ring!

"Best in Show" was won by an eight year old girl named Megan. She had come in second the year before, just behind Bob's VW, and she was NOT at all happy about that! She built a very nice sand castle with towers and a moat, and then decorated it with seaweed, shells and smooth white beach pebbles. She was MUCH happier now that she'd won first place. Megan and I are good friends, but whenever we see each other it's a little like a free fire zone with no mercy and no prisoners. We love to harass one another in every way and at every possible occasion! I went up to congratulate her on her stunning victory and artistic triumph, and then I told her that I MIGHT enter next year. She seemed very pleased to *have a bit more competition.*

"BRING IT ON!!!!!" she said "YOU haven't got a chance!"
I think Megan may be a tad more aggressive than most eight
year old girls, but this contest is all in fun anyway.

It was June of the following year, and I'd forgotten all
about sand sculptures and my little brush with Megan. I was
at the Orleans Yacht Club for a Friday night get together. This
isn't anywhere near as fancy and upscale as it sounds. Dues
are only $450 a year, and we bring all our own food to pass
and then clean up after. ISSEY, the thirteen year old daughter
of the club's Vice Commodore, saw me come in, and she came
right over to talk. This kind of social chit chat isn't very com-
mon among thirteen year old girls, so I was pretty sure she
wanted something. After a bit of small talk...

"How's school?" "Great! Except for all the classes!" ISSEY
got right to the point.

"Are you having a sand castle contest again this year?"
She asked.

"I GUESS so. I don't really know 'cause I'm not in charge,
and I don't have anything to do with it."

"IF you DO, can I enter with my best friend Isabelle?"
"ISSEY" is short for "Isabelle," so it's a good thing they came
up with different variations to their names, otherwise what-
ever she wanted was going to get confusing in a hurry.

"I'm pretty sure you have to live in Nauset Heights to en-
ter." I told her. ISSEY does NOT live anywhere near Nauset
Heights.

"YOU live in Nauset Heights, don't you?" ISSEY already
KNOWS I live in Nauset Heights, so I was starting to get a
sense of where this was going.

"Why Yes! YES INDEED! I DO happen to live in Nauset
Heights. Why might you ask?"

She was on me like dog after a squirrel, and as if being secretly summoned by a hidden sign, ISABELLE just happened to saunter by and joined in on our conversation.

"Wellllll, WE just THOUGHT maybe WE could enter as your guests IF guests are allowed. Just a thought mind you."

THAT was more than a random thought. ISSEY had done enough non- school homework to already know the contest was still on and guests were still allowed. It was two against one, so I surrendered.

"OK. You can come as my guests..."

"YEAAAAAY" they both cried in twin-like unison.

"...BUT, I have some RULES!"

The twin ISABELLES looked significantly less happy. Apparently "rules" aren't very popular among thirteen year old girls.

Who knew!

"If you REALLY want to do this, YOU have to decide what we're going to build. It has to be ALL your idea!...and you have to help with the work part too. You can't just collect your prizes and eat popsicles after."

They both agreed, and ISSEY added "and we want to WIN TOO!" They both nodded their heads furiously in agreement with themselves.

"Great! It's a deal. Just let me know next Friday night what you want to make."

The very next Friday, the two ISABELLES cornered me as soon as I walked in.

"We've DECIDED!" They announced in unison.

"And just WHAT have you decided, pray tell?" I asked.

"We want to make a SHARK!"

OH NO!, I thought, but didn't dare say. This is NOT a good choice. Everyone does sharks. There are at least four sharks every year, and they NEVER win anything! Sharks just barely qualify for the participation medal everyone gets, and you can get one of THOSE by just eating a popsicle! A shark is just a long mound of sand that's smoothed over and then has a short stubby sand bump on top for a fin.

"I don't think a shark will win." I said, hoping to change their twin minds. "How about something else?"

The two ISABELLEs stepped away and formed their own private huddle, and I desperately hoped they'd call a different play.

They broke from their huddle and lined up in front of me.

"We STILL want to do a SHARK!"

"Do you WANT to win?"

"YES!" they cried in perfect unison.

"and you STILL want to make a shark?" I said in a voice that leaked desperation.

"YES!" they said with even more determination "and we want to WIN with our shark!"

Once again, I raised the white flag and surrendered.

"OK then...a SHARK it is. I'll let you know when and where and what you need to bring."

Well, I thought after the girls had left, we can build a shark OR we can win, but we can't do both.

Two weeks later I was walking along the gravel road that runs across the top of Nauset Heights. Coming the other way toward me was Megan, my friend and upcoming sandcastle nemesis. Megan has an extremely smart mouth for a 9 year old!

"Hi, are you STILL thinking of entering the contest this year?"

That's Megan for you! Right to the heart of the matter and NO need to say what contest. We both knew!

"WELL! Hello there Megan! It's SO great to see you, and YES! Yes, I AM!" I said in my sweetest non-confrontational voice.

" SOOOOOO...Whatch'a gonna make?" She asked in a

sing- songy voice.

I should have said "NONE of your beeswax," but I didn't and that was a big mistake. Instead I told her, hoping she wasn't really listening and would just keep on walking.

"I 'm going to build a shark with two friends."

She stopped in her tracks as if she'd run into a brick wall, and she stared at me with a bug eyed look.

"A SHARK? A SHARK? You MUST be kidding! A shark is SOOOOOOO BOOOOORING!"

She drew out the word "boring" to make sure I under-stood exactly how boring a shark could be.

"You'll never win!...ANYTHING! But you wouldn't win ANYWAY, so it doesn't matter!"

"Sharks don't have to be boring." I said "and we WILL win!"

" Will NOT!!! I'll beat you AGAIN just like last year! Your sand shark is gonna be SUCH a loser!"

Megan obviously forgot that I didn't even enter last year, so I felt obliged to respond.

"I'm gonna Beat YOU like the toy drum you play with... with your friends...IF you HAD any friends...which you DON'T!"

"LOOOOOSER!" she taunted. "LOOOOOOOOOOSER!"

"Am NOT!"

"Are SO!"

"Am not! Am not ! AM NOT!!"

"Are So! Are SO! Are SO! Are so, are so, ARE SO!"

Our intellectual debate ended in a draw, so we agreed to let our sand masterpieces battle it out on the beach. Now I was in a real jam! Megan was right. Sharks are boring and will always be boring, and there was no way I'd get the two ISABELLS to change their minds. What to do? What to do? IF Megan won, I'd NEVER hear the end of it as long as she was alive, and she was ONLY NINE, so that could be a very long time! This was MOST unfortunate!

I started to think about the drawbacks with making a sand shark, and I could see three main problems. Everyone makes sharks, so they WERE in fact boring. It was impossible to make a realistic tail fin or back fin on a shark , because the sand always collapses way before they're thin enough and tall enough to look real. The best I could do was make fin shaped lumps.

Finally, there was the mouth, and this was the biggest problem. It was impossible to make a real looking OPEN mouth on a sand shark...even on a small one. It would collapse as soon as I started to make it. I could make a closed mouth with a smile and with teeth sticking out, but who wants to see a happy, smiling shark? Certainly not any judges! I wanted a shark with a HUGE, GAPING MOUTH filled with long razor sharp teeth, but THAT wasn't remotely possible. I briefly considered making the shark upside down and dead, and THAT WAY I'd be able to make an open mouth with teeth. I gave up on that idea as soon as I thought about what the crowd and the judges might say, as they gathered around my dead sand fish.

Child: "Dad, LOOK what washed up!"

Father: "Why it's a DEAD fish! I sure hope it doesn't get too hot today, because it might start to smell!"

Judge: "I think it's starting to smell already!"

No! There wouldn't be any prizes for THAT idea, and I could just hear Megan coming up to me with her first place trophy, waving it in my face, and saying:

"I see you came in DEAD last again!"

I needed to be smarter, MUCH, much smarter about this whole thing, so I took the next week to make a real plan.

Here's the plan I came up with. MY (technically OUR) shark would not be boring, because it'd be at least 20 feet long!

That would take a lot of work with big shovels, but it could be done.

I could solve the back and tail fin problem by cutting the fins out of styrofoam , painting them with wood glue and coating them with sand. That would LOOK like they're made out of sand. The mouth was harder! I had to have DENTURES, and I had no idea how to do that, but that was the ONLY way to keep the mouth from caving in. TRUE, my plan MIGHT be bending the rules just the tiniest bit, but I'd never seen any OFFICIALLY published rule book, and this WAS war.

I set about making the fins , and each one would be more than a yard high! I asked the two ISABELLES to get two tennis balls for eyes, and then paint them shiny black with red centers the size of quarters for pupils. If this was going to be a monster, then it had to look like a monster! While all this was going on, I hoped I'd stumble on some way to make the mouth. That answer came to me in early July, when I made my weekly trip to the dump. THERE IT WAS! It was sitting on the top of a pile of scrap metal just screaming "TAKE ME!" It was a gigantic commercial drier drum, with an opening a yard in diameter that had been bent into a curved half moon shape, just like a huge partially opened mouth. For the life of me, I'll never understand why anyone would ever throw such a treasure away! After a lot of effort and rope, I was able to get it into the trunk of my car and tie it tightly in place. My trunk was so open, I couldn't even see through my rear view mirror, but I made it home with NO accidents and without a single traffic ticket! So far, so good!

I put ISSEY and ISABELLE to work on the beach, gathering broken clam shells that looked like sharp jagged teeth, each one three inches long or longer. As my pile of shark teeth grew, I began to glue them into place in the mouth of the drier drum, and it was turning out to be SPECTACULAR! When it was finished, it looked like a slightly smaller version of the *jaws of a MEGALODON, the prehistoric shark that was more than 30 feet long.*

The big day finally came! The contest was set to start at 10am, but I hauled my fins, dentures and shovels down at 8 am and covered them all with tarps to avoid any prying eyes. I sure didn't want to be seen carrying all that stuff when crowds of people were around and have some busybody declare it "unsportsmanlike-like" before we even started.

The girls arrived at about 9:45. We registered and were handed our official contestant stake with flag and team number. We had a short ceremony for good luck, and then ISSEY drove it into the sand next to our pile to mark our building area.

At exactly 10am the start whistle blew, and we began shoveling to make the body, while all our "extras" remained hidden under cover. It still amazes me how quickly the two girls lost interest in shoveling and decided their time might be better spent looking for seaweed decorations, checking out our competition and checking out boys. After all, shoveling sand is such fun and SUCH good exercise! Once the rough shape of the head was done, I dragged the jaws out from under the tarp and hoisted them into place. Then all three of us covered over the drum with sand, except for its open mouth. We shoveled the rest of its 20 foot long body in place, so it connected to the head. I planted its prosthetic fins, while the two girls patted it down and smoothed the whole thing out. We even had a roller that made it look like the body was covered with scales. As a finishing touch, the two Isabells draped our shark with their seaweed jewelry. It turned out to be much better than we ever thought possible! It looked like our giant shark was lunging out of the ocean with monstrous red eyes, and its mouth wide open with razor sharp teeth ready to swallow some wayward child whole! Then we waited for the judging. I was pretty sure we'd win when one of the judges happened to pass by. He took one look at our sculpture and exclaimed "OH MY GOD. HOLY JOSEPH AND MARY!!!!" to no one in particular, but in a voice loud enough for everyone to hear. Well, at LEAST we weren't boring. Just to make sure we'd win, ISSEY and ISABELLE did the presentation telling how THEY made it, while I made myself scarce. They wanted kids to win anyway, and it WAS their idea.

We won the grand prize "BEST ON BEACH," and a second prize too, in a newly created category called "MOST UNUSUAL USE OF INDUSTRIAL MATERIALS." The girls held up their trophies and pictures were taken. Spectators then swarmed our shark and snapped endless pictures of their children being eaten by our sculpture. Megan was her usual magnanimous self in defeat, and came up to congratulate me with all the humility she could muster.

"You CHEATED!" She exclaimed.

"Megan!" I said, putting on my most pained expression. "My feelings are totally CRUSHED! How could you EVER say such a HURTFUL thing?"

"BECAUSE it's TRUE! You used fake fins and made a fake mouth out of a clothes dryer, and THAT'S cheating because they aren't made of sand!"

I pointed out that she had decorated her sand castle with seaweed, shells and sea pebbles.

"Technically, those things aren't sand either!"

She didn't appreciate my logic, and said "but THEY'RE allowed 'cause they washed up on the beach."

Once again I had to point out her faulty logic.

"Styrofoam and metal containers wash up on the beach all the time. How do YOU know my stuff didn't wash up just like yours?"

Megan wasn't at all satisfied with my answers, and she pointed to her eyes with two fingers, squinted and then said .

"I'll be WATCHING YOU!" and then added "I'm gonna tell

the judges to make SURE that using major household appliances is STRICTLY ILLEGAL next year!" and she turned to leave. I couldn't let her go on such a sad note, NOT after losing like that.

"MEGAN!" I called after her "Guess WHAT?"

She turned around, "What?"

"I'm gonna cheat AGAIN next year too, JUST for you!"

The next year, when I saw Megan again, things picked up pretty much where we'd left off.

"SOOOOO! Whacha gonna make THIS year!" She asked.

"NONE of your bees wax! It's highly confidential! In fact it's HIGHLY CLASSIFIED! It's SO top secret, that I don't even know! BUT, when I do find out, I'm SURE I'll win!"

In truth, I'd already decided that I WOULDN'T enter this year, but I didn't want Megan to know that.

The day of the contest came. I had a clipboard with a pen and paper, and I walked down to where Megan's flag was planted. She was building what looked like another one of her elegant sand castles. She was getting much better at it, and she was busily carving turrets and bridges with a knife and scooping out a moat with a spoon. I sat down near her flag and started writing.

After a while, she looked up.

"WHAT are you doing?" She asked, and then added "WHATEVER it is, you better not be using any illegal stuff!"

"Megan, I absolutely and totally PROMISE I won't use anything YOU wouldn't use!" And I kept writing on my clipboard.

"What ARE you making anyway?"

I looked up from my writing and said "I'm going to make EXACTLY what you're making! Only BIGGER! MUCH, MUCH BIGGER, but I need to make SURE I copy everything down

JUST right, so don't mind ME! Pay NO attention to ME!
Just keep on working, so I can finish writing it ALL down!"
Megan looked at me with disbelief, and for the very first
time in her young life, she was at a loss for words.
She was speechless. because she was torn between rat-
ting me out to the judges or tattling on me to her mother.
Finally, she decided! "MOMMMMEEEE!" She yelled!

When you create something, it can be very hard to make it special and to make it really stand out. It has to have "TEETH" to capture the attention of your audience.

I'm ready to write my research report, but I need more! I HAVE to PROVE that the PROOF RESTRIKE 1838-O's were made on the night of March 27, 1839, and I HAVE to be able to say WHY they were made! These will be the "teeth" for my presentation, but I haven't found them yet. IF I can find them, at least my research report won't be boring!

30

Finding Lost Letters

IN INTERNET TREASURE HUNTING, you've got to narrow your target and become the world's expert on your new narrow target. You've got to know more about it than anyone else, and a funny thing happens when you do this. Not only do you know more, you also know better than anyone else WHAT to look for and WHERE TO LOOK. Now that we've solved the essential mystery of the 1838-O half dollar, it's fair to say that WE are now the experts, and WE will know best where to find any other missing pieces to this puzzle. The other "experts" don't even know what pieces are missing, let alone where to look because they don't see the new picture.

There are only two key pieces left to find. The first is to PROVE that all the other 8 specimens were struck on the night of March 27. The GR-1 die crack has already proven that's the case for the Smithsonian specimen, because it was made at the same time as the PROOF 1839's, and the 1839 dies weren't available before that date. The GR-1 die crack ALSO proves that no 1838-O half dollars or 1839-O PROOFS (4-5 coins) were made AFTER the night of March 27, because all known circulation strike 1839-O's have a bigger GR-1 die cracks. Their production began very late on the night of March 27 or on March 28. While it's highly likely that all 7 other Proof Restrikes were made at that same time, it IS remotely possible they could have been made earlier, IF Tyler had fixed the large dollar press after its January collapse. In order to PROVE that ALL the restrikes were made on the night of March 27, we only need to prove that Tyler didn't fix the large press before that date.

The second piece we need to find is WHY the New Orleans Mint made 10 PROOF RESTRIKES on the night of March 27, and then sent them to the very person who ordered that they NEVER BE MADE!

The experts believe only 4-5 were made, and this was done at Mint Director Patterson's written request, but that letter has been lost.

In searching for any new information about fixing the large coin press, that information would have to come from archival letters. The good news is that this is exactly the kind of thing that would be mentioned in a "status report" letter. The bad news is that noted Numismatic researcher, R.W.Julian, has combed through ALL the archival letters from the Philadelphia and New Orleans Mints for that time period. Those letters are in the Philadelphia Mint Archives, and he found NOTHING even hinting at a repair of the broken dollar press and a second productions of proof restrikes. The archival letters only mentioned the first January 1839 production run of half dollars for circulation and the collapse of the reverse die that ended that run. There is virtually no chance that he missed anything in his exhaustive searches. The conclusion right now is that if any letters did exist, they must have been lost. There also should have been letters that mention the shipping of those restrikes to Patterson and their receipt, but apparently, those have been lost as well.

Since WE are now the experts, we can take another look at the letters we DO have, and they provide a very interesting clue. We have a regular flow of archival letters between Mint Director Patterson, New Orleans Branch Mint Superintendent Bradford and Chief Coiner Tyler for the period January 15, 1839 through March 29 1839. Then they just stop! There are NO more letters between these three people until June 13. It's very odd that the letters involving just THOSE people should ALL be lost during that period. It would seem to be beyond the bounds of coincidence. But, there IS something else! There was a major conflict between Tyler and Bradford at that time. This conflict had escalated to the point where Bradford wanted to fire Tyler, and he had written the Secretary of the Treasury to conduct an investigation. An investigation was done, sworn testimony taken from the people involved, and a judgement rendered. Tyler kept HIS job, but BRADFORD WAS FIRED! The firing of the Branch Mint Superintendent is no small matter, and it would have to have been approved by the Secretary of the Treasury, if not the President of the United States himself! A case like this would DEMAND an evidentiary file, and THAT FILE would surely contain letters between all the people involved...PATTERSON, BRADFORD and TYLER. What's more, those letters would have been taken FROM the Philadelphia Mint Archives as evidence and wouldn't have been returned. They would've been kept in the evidentiary file in Washington.

It is highly likely that there are files located in some other Archives containing some of the missing letters from that exact time period, but no one's ever looked for them. It's just a long shot idea, but we know exactly what to look for, and the folks at the National Archives should know exactly where to look!

I go on the National Archives website and type in a VERY specific search request. "Do you have any files relating to the 1839 investigation of the New Orleans Branch Mint Superintendent David Bradford and Chief Coiner Rufus Tyler? If you do, WHERE are they located?"

The result of this short request is very interesting. I receive an e mail two weeks later that says my request has been forwarded to a person who MIGHT know, and then that was forwarded to another who SHOULD know. Finally, my request reaches Mr Tab Lewis, who works in "Textual Reference Operations" at the National Archives in College Park, Maryland, and he DOES know! Mr. Lewis writes me that they HAVE the files, the files contain letters from Patterson, Bradford and Tyler, and he gives me the exact reference numbers to access those files. They don't have the time or resources to conduct the search themselves, but I can hire someone or visit the archives and do the search myself.

This is VERY good news, and it was very likely that NO ONE has ever looked through these "lost" letters. It reminds me of the end of the movie "Raiders of the Lost Ark," when the ARK is put into a Government warehouse where it will NEVER be found again!

The College Park Archives website also has a list of researchers that you can contact to hire for your search. Every time I access the list, the names come up in a different order. I guess this is for "fairness," because if your name happens to be Aaanderson, you'd get all the search business. When you pull up a name, it gives a brief summary of his or her area of expertise. I go through about ten names, and it isn't encouraging. Most specialize in Native American research, and no one has ever done any Numismatic research. I finally select three names to contact who seem to do more general research, and I e mail all of them. Their responses are all the same. They're not interested, because they only do long term projects for Corporations or for people writing books, AND they all charge more than $100 an hour! Either I do this search myself, or I don't do it at all!

In late April 2016, we will drive from Savannah back to Cape Cod again for the summer, and College Park Maryland is not too much out of the way. I set up an appointment with Tab Lewis at the National Archives for 9am on Monday May 1, 2016.

I really want to do this entire treasure hunt without leaving my house, so this side trip will be the one exception. We'll have to leave the Archives by 12:30 pm at the very latest, so we can make another late afternoon meeting 200 miles away with John Albanese. John is founder of CAC, a coin certification company, and he's one of the most respected Numismatists in the world. I want to get his CAC endorsement on the CINDERELLA COIN in it's new holder AND talk to him about my research findings. This is a meeting that CAN'T be missed. I'll have to bring the coin with me, and that makes me extremely nervous but there's no choice!

At 8am on May 1, Patti and I leave the Hampton Inn on the University of Maryland campus and drive to the COLLEGE PARK ARCHIVES. It's only about ten minutes away, but the check-in and registration process could be a bit complicated, and THIS is a new experience for us. The actual archives open at exactly 9 am, and I want to be FIRST in line. It could be a very long morning at the archives! There's no telling how many letters there are and how long it'll take to go through them, so I decide to start with just the letters dated between March 1st and June 15, 1839. I'll bring a peanut butter sandwich and a Diet Coke with me, so I can work right through lunch without taking a break!

This place has security everywhere! Our car is checked at the first gate, and I tell the guard we have an appointment with Mr. Lewis. Our car is checked again, and this guard tells us where to park. There's another guard at the front door, and once inside we have to go through scanners. Patti goes first and has no problems, but I'm not nearly so lucky! I place everything I have on the conveyer belt, including my shoes. Just to be sure we're in the right place, I check the signs. YEP! We're OK! We're at the National Archives and not the CIA. The body scanner buzzes angrily and persistently like I've stepped on a bees' nest as I walk through.

"PLEASE BACK UP, SIR, and try it again!"

I explain to the guard that I have a metal hip, so there isn't much point in trying it again, unless he just likes to hear the buzzing sound. He reluctantly agrees, and I get a hand pat down instead. During all this, my lunch finally makes it through the scanner, and another guard in a very official looking uniform signals me to come over. He holds up my paper bag with two fingers, as if it contained a three day old fish.

"WHAT are you planning to DO with THIS?" he asks.

"That's just my lunch. I'm going to take it up to the archive reading room and eat it, while I go through all the old letters with Mr. Lewis."

"PEANUT BUTTER AND JELLY?" He asks in a tone tinged with disbelief.

"Why YES! My favorite! AND a bottle of Diet Coke for when I get thirsty." I had no idea their scanners were THAT good!

The guard was still holding my bag in his "dead fish" pose, even though he knew it was just my lunch.

"I'm sorry Sir, it DOESN'T work that way. NO food OR drink is allowed in the reading room. You'll have to take it downstairs and put it in a locker along with everything else you have here."

In a futile attempt to try to justify their draconian rules he adds, "Archival papers and peanut butter and jelly DON'T mix very well." For a brief moment I was tempted to ask about my Diet Coke, but I already knew that probably wouldn't mix well either.

"Can I get some of the letters and bring them down here while I eat lunch?"

"No!" He says in a slightly less friendly tone. "NOTHING leaves the reading room. When you're ready to go up to the reading room, you'll have to get a photo ID badge first, and then store all your belongings... AND that includes your lunch! The elevator will take you up when it opens at 9am."

Patti and I fill out the identification and background forms and we're first in line. We received our ID's, which are only good for today.

"I'm mildly surprised they don't fingerprint us and do an FBI background check." Patti gave me a look that said the whole process might be faster if I kept my thoughts to myself.

We store all our things in the lockers downstairs. I go to stand by the elevators, while she finds a comfortable chair in the lobby where she can read, while I search the archives.

There's another scanner leading to the elevators, and it doesn't like my metal hip anymore than the first.

At last, I'm heading up to the archives, and I'd get my chance to see the lost letters.

The elevators doors open, and I find myself in a different world. Metal tables are spread out in a checkerboard pattern in a huge open room. To my right is a long desk where I'd present my written request with document locator numbers. The archival attendants would take each request, process it and then place it in a holder in the order it was received. Other attendants would take each request along with a wheeled cart and then vanish into the vast multi -story archival library behind the service desk. It's like a giant anthill, with endless carts disappearing into the tunnels behind the desk and other carts streaming out filled with dusty volumes and files. The filled carts are parked at the entrance of the service area, and the name of the person who requested the files is posted on a board. That is your signal to go up and take the cart to your work table. I go to the service desk and ask for Tab Lewis. He is in his office on the immediate right of the elevators, and he's expecting me. He had already filled out the document request forms and gives them to me. I thank him, go back to the service desk and give them to the young lady who steps forward to help.

"I've never done this before. What happens now?" I ask.

"Just wait until your name is posted and your cart is out. Then you can take it to your table and start working. When you're all done, you just put the material back in the cart and bring it back over here, along with this check out and return slip. That way we will know exactly what you're returning, so we can check it off and make sure it's returned to it's proper place. You'll get TWO file boxes, so you'll get TWO slips. In the meantime, you can just wait at your table."

It all seemed very orderly and very Clear!

"How long will it take to bring out my files?" I ask, hoping it wouldn't be more than 15 minutes since I was her first customer.

"You're slotted for delivery at 10! The way it works is your delivery comes in the next hour AFTER you submit your request."

It's only 9:15. I've got some time to kill, so I find a table and make myself comfortable. I know I'd be a whole lot more comfortable with my peanut butter and jelly sandwich and with my Diet Coke, but it's too late for that. The tables start to fill up as people exit the elevator and claim their work space. I talk to a few nearby while we wait, and all of them are writing historical books of one kind or another. They come every day, spend all day, and leave when the Archives close.

The carts loaded with dusty folders, stacks of books and binders start to emerge from the anthill behind the service desk and names are being posted. Somehow, each person seems instinctively to know when their cart is ready for pick up. They never even look at the posted list of names. They just go right to their cart, wheel it to their table, lift one box or file out and begin working. This goes on for a half hour, and by now the same people have made multiple trips returning carts and picking up new ones. NOTHING for me yet!

By 10am, I go to the service desk and ask. I WAS the very first person to put in a request, so I'm starting to get worried. Their answer doesn't make me feel any better. Apparently, undelivered requests at closing last Friday are moved to the head of the line on Monday. My request will be brought out SOMETIME during the 10 o'clock hour, which means some time before 11am. I finally get my cart at 10:45, and it's clear I'm not going to have enough time to really study all this stuff carefully, so I'll have to do some triage and focus on just most likely letters. I've got TWO HOURS to get this done before I have to leave.

I reach in and take out a bundle of letters dated May 16, 1839 through June 16, 1839. I'll work backwards through May, April and March and go as far as I can. I feel a twinge of optimism as I look at the first bundle. They're tied up with a very old ribbon which hasn't been untied for more than a hundred years. The knot is so tight, I can't even begin to untie it. There's only one answer, so I'm off to the service desk. After all, THAT'S what a service desk is for.

"Do you have scissors and maybe some scotch tape I can borrow for a moment?"

My request was met with a look of sheer panic. You'd think I was at the National Aquarium and had asked to borrow a fishing pole and some bait. One of the attendants was apoplectic that I still had the bundle of letters in my hand, while the other had nearly fainted at my request for scissors and tape. For just a moment, I thought if I fanned her with my bundle of letters, that might help her recover, but I never got that far.

"THOSE!" She said, pointing at the bundle in my hand "are NEVER, EVER, TO LEAVE YOUR WORK AREA!"

Now that she was sufficiently recovered to speak, the other one chimed in, "SISSORS AND TAPE are NEVER, EVER permitted in the National Archives Reading Room!"

I pleaded ignorance of the law, begged for mercy and showed them the Gordian knot that was keeping me from my work. Their wrath dissipated instantly, and they both leaned over and peered intently at the knotted ribbon as if it was a new species of insect that had just crawled out from some of their disintegrating manuscripts.

"Sir, perhaps we can solve this WITHOUT scissors and tape!"

She carefully slid the old ribbon back and forth ever so slightly without bending the letters, and in about five minutes it was finally off. She added helpfully, "You can put it back on the same way." I thank them profusely for this bit of remarkable insight that never occurred to me.

I COULD, but in truth that ribbon was going to go back on in about five SECONDS, and I'd make darned sure they weren't watching when I did it.

BACK TO MY DESK, and I was finally going to start! The first letter in the bundle has the date May 16, 1839 and it's from Rufus Tyler to Robert Patterson the Mint Director. THIS is VERY GOOD start, and I carefully unfold the ancient paper.

"WHAT language is this thing written in? Sanskrit? Rongo-Rongo? CIA Code?" I think to myself as I stare in disbelief at what's now in front of me.

I wasn't going to READ these letters, I was going to have to TRANSLATE them!

In 2006, I decided to climb Mount Kilimanjaro and I flew to Nairobi, Kenya as the first step in my adventure. I was going to "rough it" all the way, so I spent the night in a local hotel and then got up early to catch the bus to Moshe, Tanzania. The bus was scheduled to leave PROMPTLY at 8am and it wouldn't wait. It was an eight hour trip, and there was only one bus each day. I had my reservation, and I was sitting on the bench at the bus stop with all my climbing gear at exactly 7am. I was a full hour early, but I didn't want to take any chances.

At 7:45, I was filled with excitement. The bus was about to arrive and my great adventure was just about to begin!

At 8am, my excitement was beginning to turn into

concern. Where was the bus? Why weren't there any other people waiting for the bus? Was I in the wrong place?

By 8:30, my minor concerns had started to grow into the very mountain I was planning to climb. I tried asking some local people but they just shrugged their shoulders.

At about 8:45, a young Canadian girl arrived and sat down in the bench next to me. Since she also had a backpack and climbing poles, I took a wild shot in the dark.

"Are you going to Climb Kilimanjaro?" I asked.

" Yes! But I've never climbed anything like this before. How about you?"

"Me too, and Me too! It's almost 20,000 feet, and I'm sort of nervous about it. Do you know when the bus is suppose to come?"

Her name was Jihan, and she said, "They told me it's a bit irregular. It comes when it comes!"

At 9:15, the bus arrived, and three "drivers" got out. One was the actual driver, one checked tickets and one seemed to be in charge of crowd control. I handed my ticket to Mr. ticket man, who was immediately joined by Mr. crowd control, and they both studied my ticket intently.They seemed satisfied, and Mr Ticket pulled out a clipboard and said "Now WHO are you, and WHERE are you going?"

I spelled out my name and told him I was going to Moshe. He carefully wrote my name and destination in the very first space at the top of his paper. Jihan did the same, and we both moved to get on the bus but were waived off by Mr. Crowd control, so we sat back down on our bench.

At about 9:30, more people arrived, but it was clear there weren't any more climbers. I suspected they were "local," especially the heavy set lady carrying a basket of chickens. Climbing Kilimanjaro with a basket of chickens on her head seemed MOST unlikely. Mr. Ticket came back and asked "Now WHO are you, and WHERE are you going?"

We both repeated our stories, and he nodded gravely as he listened.

At 9:45, we were allowed to get on the bus. Jihan and I sat together at the front with our equipment in the opposite seat. The lady with her chickens sat behind us, and either the lady or the chickens started nervously clucking.

At 10:15, Mr. Crowd control stepped back on the bus with the clipboard and asked us "Now WHO are you, and WHERE are you going?" This time I didn't answer. Instead, I just pointed to the first two names at the top of his list, hoping that sign language would work better than English.

At 10:30, Mr crowd control, Mr ticket AND Mr. DRIVER all got in the bus, and Mr. Driver started the engine.

We were FINALLY off on our great adventure. The bus drove a total of 11 feet and pulled into the gas station that was right next to our bench. All the Mr's got out to check a new bunch of travelers and to gas up the bus. Who would have guessed that two different bus stops would be only 11 feet apart.

At 10:45, the bus left that station and went 100 yards to another stop, and then to another and then to another.

Finally at 11:00, we were leaving Nairobi. The bus picked up speed which was a new experience, so we knew we were on our way at last. Suddenly, Mr Driver jammed on the brakes and brought his bus to a screeching halt on what was a gravel road in the middle of the jungle. The were no houses, no gas stations and no people around.

Mr. crowd control got off, and vanished into the underbrush while our bus remained parked with its door wide open.

"What NOW?" I said to Jihan. She rolled her eyes, but said nothing.

After 5 more minutes, Mr. Control returned with 3 ears of still steaming roasted corn, two of which he handed to his buddies. We sat there while they ate their roasted ears of corn.

Sometimes, everything seems to conspire to keep you from starting a project.

As I sit looking at the faded lines that try to pass as handwriting, I feel like I'm back in the bus going from Nairobi to Moshe.

No more ROASTED CORN! It's time to decipher these scribblings, and this could take weeks! I only have two hours, so the only thing I can do now is scan the letters for a few key words like "half dollar," "50 cents," "coins" and "minting." I can easily spot those words even though Tyler's writing is nearly impossible to read, and then I can take the time to decipher the few sentences that have those words. There's nothing in the first letter, or in the second, third, fourth or fifth. The last letter in this bundle is from Tyler to New Orleans Superintendent Bradford, and I can dismiss it quickly, because it's a coinage production summary and mostly a bunch of numbers. It does mention "half dollar" production, but it states that FUTURE production will be doubled in the last half of the year. Nothing there, because my focus is on production of half dollars before April 1.

Now that the first packet is done, I take out a second bundle with another old blue ribbon around it. I start to slide the ribbon off, when three uniformed guards rush up to my table.

I know I'm in big trouble, but they haven't pulled out their guns YET!

"WHAT have I done NOW?" I ask, as I raise both hands in surrender.

The swat team leader says in his sternest voice, "You took out TWO bundles at ONCE," as he quickly points to my first bundle on the table and the second I'd just taken out. " YOU NEVER, EVER take out TWO bundles at once! You HAVE to put the first one back in the archive box with THIS file card marking its proper location!"

He drew out a long file card like a Samurai warrior, and waved it in front of all the swat team members who dutifully bowed in agreement. They're all heavily armed with file cards and ready to respond to any emergency.

"I'm SORRY! I didn't know!"

My words don't have the desired effect, as each of the guards points in a different direction, where there are large signs saying "You MUST re-turn each item to your archive box before removing another. FILE CARDS are available at reception for marking item location in your file box."

The signs are everywhere, so I raise my hands in surrender again, wondering if I'm going to be taken to an interrogation room, or just kicked out of the building.

The swat leader says, "THAT's not necessary, but make sure you follow proper procedures from now on!"

The guards leave and return to their hidden observation/sniper post where ever that is, and I go back to my translation work.

NOTHING !

NOTHING !

NOTHING !

And NOTHING !

Two hours go by, and I'm all the way back to March 1, 1839. There are lots of letters, but not one mentions the production, shipping or receiving of the 10 proof RESTRIKE half dollars. There should be some letters, but there are NONE! I'd come up completely empty. The only good news is that Patti hadn't eaten my peanut butter and jelly sand-wich yet. We stop at a WENDY's for a quick lunch and my sandwich stayed in its bag as an emergency provision. For the next two hours I gripe about not finding anything.

"It just doesn't make sense. I KNOW they made 10 RESTRIKE PROOFS on the night of March 27. There HAS to be a letter that tells about mak-ing and shipping the coins! There HAS to be a letter from Patterson that mentions receiving the coins. He was SO strict about "accountability of assets." He'd NEVER let something like that pass. The New Orleans Mint even wrote him when they put a couple of half dimes into the corner-stone of their new Mint building! That's just 10 cents!"

Patti just listens to my continuous rant, and then finally she says, "Maybe they didn't make them that night. You SAID you hadn't abso-lutely proven that part."

She's right! I haven't proven that part...BUT there's something else. Then it dawns on me! I'd been so focused on the making and shipping of the coins, the repair of the large coin press had slipped my mind.

The last letter in the first bundle was a summary of Tyler's coinage production, and he wrote that he'd now be able to DOUBLE the number of half dollars BECAUSE he had just FIXED THE LARGE PRESS! This is a HUGE breakthrough! Theories will always remain just theories, but PROOF is different. PROOF becomes HISTORY!

With THAT one letter, I can now PROVE that all other 1838-O AND the 4-5 proof 1839-O half dollars were made on the night of March 27. They couldn't have been made any earlier, because there was no coining press available to make them earlier. He hadn't fixed the large press yet. They couldn't have been made any later based on the extent of their GR-1 die cracks! That's wonderful news, BUT I don't have a copy of the letter, and I didn't even write down its specific reference number. I'm going to have to find a way to get a copy.

We continue on and meet with John Albanese, and that turns out to be more good news. He looks at my half dollar and tells me he knows it well. He says "It's SO obvious that the reverse dentil grooves were made by the collapsed reverse die, it's not even worth discussing!" He then advises me NEVER to call them "marks," because they're part of the minting process and not made by something else.

Once we get to our beach house, the issue of getting a copy of the letter is still on my mind, so I send an e Mail to Tab Lewis at the College Park Archives. I get an e Mail back fro Mr. Lewis about 2 weeks later, and he's gone way, way beyond the call of duty! He's attached a copy of the missing letter.

APRIL 16, 1839 FROM MR. TYLER TO MR. BRADFORD

"The large coining press now being in successful operation will of course double the amount of coinage IN BALANCE with the same count of labor."
My PROOF that all the PROOF RESTRIKES were made on the night of March 27 is now complete!
"THANK YOU, MR.LEWIS!"

31

Schrödinger Smells a Rat!

SO HERE WE ARE, nearly at the end of our treasure hunt. The Cinderella Coin did prove to be the key piece needed to complete the puzzle. It did turn out to be the black Panther Head piece, with its golden eyes staring back but mostly hidden in the jungle.

We now know that none of the surviving 1838-O half dollars were ever produced in Philadelphia. We now know that 10 CIRCULATION STRIKE coins were produced in January 1839 on written orders from the Mint Director.

We now know that there is ONLY ONE survivor from that original circulation run, and that survivor is THE CINDERELLA COIN.

We now know that 10 PROOF RESTRIKES were made on the night of March 27, 1939.

Finally, we know that these 10 PROOF RESTRIKES were sent to the Mint Director in Philadelphia.

THESE are all proven facts, but we don't know why. WHY WOULD THE NEW ORLEANS MINT VIOLATE DIRECT WRITTEN ORDERS, AND THEN SEND THE TEN RESTRIKES TO THE VERY PERSON WHO ORDERED THAT THEY NEVER BE MADE? WHY IS THERE NO RECORD OF THE PRODUCTION OR SHIPMENT OF THESE 10 COINS?

We've finally solved the 1838-O mystery that's confounded Numismatist for 180 years, but I can't write the research report without some explanation for WHY this was done. These are the teeth to my report, and I badly need teeth!

Once again, these few remaining pieces of the puzzle still swirl around my head, but they never link up! They just keep swirling around in a nonsensical swarm.

It seems my mind keeps working on problems, even when I'm asleep. My first year at Groton, my Geometry teacher, Mr.Smith, gave our class a very hard problem to solve for the next day. I was middle good at math on my very best day, but even the top students couldn't solve this problem. That night I went to bed, and I saw the entire solution written out in my dream. It was fresh in my mind when I woke up, so I wrote it out, AND IT WAS RIGHT! No one else even came close to solving the problem.

I finally fall asleep, and in my restless sleep, I have a dream, but in THIS dream there's no table and no puzzle. I'm in my room, and there's a knock on my door. I know it can't be Schrödinger, because cats can't knock. I open the door, and there is Mr. Spock, the Vulcan of Star Trek fame. Mr. Spock has Schrödinger cradled in his arms, and Schrödinger seems quite content.

Mr Spock looks at me, and says "ILLOGICAL! MOST ILLOGICAL!"

"WHAT'S illogical?" I ask.

Mr. Spock arches his right eyebrow in a look of surprise.

"Why, it's ILLOGICAL that the New Orleans Mint should MAKE half dollars after being ordered NOT to do so. MOST illogical!"

Schrödinger starts squirming and Spock puts him down, and he immediately sets off exploring, as if looking for a mouse.

"BUT, they DID make the coins, and they DID send them! I've proven that!"

Mr Spock seems even more surprised at my response. In the background, there's a clanging and banging of pots and pans. Schrödinger is chasing something bigger than a mouse. He's after a rat!

Mr Spock answers, "I never SAID the New Orleans Mint didn't MAKE the coins, and I never SAID they didn't SEND the coins. I merely stated that it was MOST ILLOGICAL that they did so."

"I DON'T UNDERSTAND!" I cry.

Mr Spock now holds a communicator in his hand. He lifts it to his mouth and says, "MR SCOTT, Beam me up IMMEDIATELY! I fear that such stupidity may be infectious!"

There's a buzzing with wavy lights. Mr. Spock vanishes, and I wake up.

I hope that my dream has some kind of clue like in Geometry, but whatever it is, it's not at all obvious to me, so I go back to sleep.

The next morning, I'm still thinking about the dream and Mr. Spock. He was right. It was illogical, and yet it HAD happened!

I know it's illogical, so there's nothing new in that, but THEN things start to come together. It was illogical that the New Orleans Mint MADE coins that they were directly ordered NOT to make, but it's MORE than that! They made the coins almost immediately after getting Patterson's order NOT to make them, AND they made exactly 10, the same number as were produced in the original run. Then I finally see it! Mr. Spock WAS right ! It was illogical for the New Orleans Mint to MAKE them, but it wasn't illogical for New Orleans to SEND them. Bradford believed he had to send back the 10 original circulation coins, just like he believed he had to send back the original dies. If Tyler no longer had those coins, he'd have to MAKE new replacements to send, otherwise he'd be fired!

Years ago, when I was living in Brighton Australia, I decided to spend a Saturday morning at the beach. I wandered down, spread out my blanket, and soon I was half asleep. Before long two children came down, and they spread out their things close by. The girl was about seven, and she was clearly in charge of her younger brother. She told him where to put his things, and he dutifully did everything she told him. When they were finally settled, the older girl put her hands on her hips and then announced, "NOW we're going to have a sandcastle building contest...and I will be the JUDGE!"

Her little brother looked down at his feet, and then looked up at her.

"Ok." He said, "But you CAN'T vote for yourself!"

What's completely illogical for one person may be entirely logical for another.

Rufus Tyler and Superintendent Bradford were in serious conflict. Bradford wanted him fired and had written to Secretary of Treasury Levi Woodbury asking for an investigation. On March 29, Bradford wrote Patterson that he had given his direct order to Tyler that the dies of 1838 "BE NOT USED BY YOU!" He wanted to clean up all the loose ends involving the 1838 half dollars, so he also wrote that he wanted to return the dies to Philadelphia. This timing is all wrong, and I smell a rat!

NOW, I can SEE the rat, and Schrödinger was chasing it in my dream. We've already PROVEN that Tyler made the 10 Proofs on the night of March 27, but Bradford had talked to Tyler before March 27 and believed that no more 1838 half dollars had, or ever would be made. BRADFORD DIDN'T KNOW THAT TYLER HAD ALREADY MADE THE 10 PROOFS WHEN HE WROTE HIS MARCH 29 LETTER TO PATTERSON. This proves that Tyler made the coins despite being ordered not to, and that he made them in secret. He made them at NIGHT, when no one would be around to see what he was doing, AND he left no written trace of his secret production run.

BRADFORD'S MARCH 29, 1839 LETTER ABSOLUTELY PROVES THAT HE DID NOT KNOW TYLER HAD ALREADY PRODUCED THE PROOF RESTRIKES!

WHY DID TYLER DO THIS? HE DID IT TO SAVE HIS JOB! Returning or destroying the 1838 dies was just one action required to meet Patterson's order. The other action was to deal with the 10 original coins Tyler made in January. Patterson knew the New Orleans Mint had 10 original circulation coins, so something had to be done with them. They couldn't be distributed like 1839 half dollars, and they couldn't be held at the New Orleans Mint. They couldn't even be destroyed, unless they got a direct order to do so from Patterson. There can be no doubt that Bradford told Tyler to RETURN THE 10 ORIGINAL CIRCULATION STRIKES TO PATTERSON. That was the easiest solution by far, but Tyler no longer had the coins to return. Given his conflict with Bradford, Tyler knew that he'd be fired for the "loss" of this officially minted coinage. Tyler decided to make the highest quality PROOFS as replacements, because he knew the returned coins would be seen and examined by both the Secretary of Treasury and the Mint Director. Their high PROOF quality would reflect well on his work.

Finally, the puzzle is complete, and the picture is clear! We now understand why this has remained an unsolved mystery for 180 years. It was always suppose to be a secret, because it was an ILLEGAL action taken in direct violation of written and verbal orders from both the Director of the US Mint and the Superintendent of the New Orleans Mint. Tyler's 10 PROOF RESTRIKES were illegally made, and only the physical characteristics of the coins themselves could reveal the truth.

There is just one final piece to this story. We now know why there's no written record of the Illegal production of replacements on the night of March 27, BUT the whole purpose was to send these restrikes to Patterson as REPLACEMENTS. There HAS to be some record of Patterson receiving a shipment of coins from the New Orleans Mint around this time, but nothing has ever been found in the Philadelphia Mint Archives. Since we're now the world's expert on the 1838-O half dollar, WE know better than anyone else what to look for and WHERE to look.

WHAT are we looking for? Branch mint coins were shipped in an ASSAY BOX for security and accountability control, so we're looking for a letter from Patterson that mentions receiving an assay box with coin samples from New Orleans.

WHEN would this letter have been written ? It's likely that Bradford would have wanted the whole 1838 half dollar " directive " wrapped up all at the same time to avoid any confusion. We HAVE a letter dated June 13, 1839 from Bradford to Patterson that details the WITNESSED

DESTRUCTION of the 1838 half dollar dies, so it's most likely Patterson would have received the assay box sometime between May 15 and June 15.

WHO would the letter be from? The assay box would have been sent from New Orleans by Bradford to Secretary of Treasury Woodbury. After reviewing its contents, Woodbury would have sent it on to Patterson. The letter we're looking for should be FROM Patterson TO Secretary of Treasury Woodbury stating that he'd received the assay box.

WHERE would this letter be located if it exists? It would be in the archival files of the Secretary of the Treasury.

Since the location, author and date of the letter I'm looking for is so tightly defined, I hope that Tab Lewis may be be able to help me out once again!

I send Mr.Lewis another email and hope for the best!

Two weeks later, Mr. Lewis comes through again, and he sends me a letter from Patterson to Woodbury dated June 4, 1839. The very first line reads as follows:

"Sir, the box from the New Orleans Mint containing assay pieces (coins) and forwarded by you on the 31st ult (of last month) has come safely to hand."
THANK YOU AGAIN, MR LEWIS!

32

Cinderella Is a Princess!

NOW OUR INTERNET treasure hunt is over. Did we find a treasure?

When we started, the ANDERSON DUPONT 1838-O half dollar didn't even deserve a footnote in the world of coin collecting . It had no history earlier than the 1954 Anderson DuPont auction, which gave it its name. It had no PROVENANCE!

Like Cinderella, it has a black soot-covered appearance. It's been called " an abraided (damaged) Proof", "artificially discolored", "dirty," "a worn pocket piece" and "an affordable option" for any collector who wanted an 1838-O regardless of condition. By contrast, her eight PROOF 1838-O sisters had razor sharp strikes, beautiful mirror-like finishes and were dressed in radiant gowns of gold, lavender, blue and lilac toning. She was TRULY the poorest of step sisters.

BUT, just like the Cinderella story, there was a glass slipper. That glass slipper was the reverse half dollar die used to strike the original coins for circulation in January 1839. For years, all the experts tried to get Cinderella's beautiful sisters to fit into that glass slipper, but it NEVER WORKED, no matter how hard they tried. In all that time, they NEVER tried the slipper on the Cinderella Coin, and so the controversy raged on with ever new theories being put forward and ever more books being written.

When Cinderella finally tried on the slipper, it fit perfectly, and all at once her true identity was revealed.

The Cinderella coin is:

THE ONLY SURVIVING COIN FROM THE SHORTEST US CIRCULATION RUN EVER MADE.

THE ONLY SURVIVING ORIGINAL 1838-O HALF DOLLAR.

THE ONLY SURVIVING CIRCULATION STRIKE 1838-O HALF DOLLAR.

THE EARLIEST KNOWN LARGE SILVER COIN EVER MADE AT ANY BRANCH MINT.

HISTORICALLY, THE MOST IMPORTANT BRANCH MINT COIN EVER STRUCK.

and there's more!

ALL OTHER KNOWN 1838-O HALF DOLLARS ARE SPECIFICALLY PROHIBITED PROOF RESTRIKES.

ALL OTHER 1838-O HALF DOLLARS WERE ILLEGALLY STRUCK IN SECRET ON THE NIGHT OF MARCH 27, 1839.

CINDERELLA IS THE ONLY LEGALLY AUTHORIZED AND LEGALLY PRODUCED 1838-O HALF DOLLAR.

All this has been absolutely proven, and it's unprecedented in the world of US Numismatics. There have been UNAUTHORIZED productions, like the 1913 Liberty Nickel. There have been coins that were legally minted but illegally distributed (stolen), like the 1933 $20 gold double eagle. There have been coins minted at a much later date than the date on the coin itself, like the 1804 silver dollar. Finally, there have been very rare US coins that were made just for collectors with no intention of ever making them for circulation. Many of these coins are extraordinarily rare, but there has NEVER been a case like this, where SPECIFIC WRITTEN ORDERS WERE GIVEN BY THE DIRECTOR OF THE US MINT THAT THESE COIN MUST NEVER BE MADE, AND DESPITE THESE ORDERS, THE COINS WERE ILLEGALLY MADE IN SECRET AT NIGHT.

The CINDERELLA COIN is not just A Princess! She is THE princess! She is the rarest U.S. circulation strike ever made and one of the greatest treasures in all of American Numismatics!

33

The Fainting Lady

WHILE THIS BOOK tells the story of the CINDERELLA COIN, it's important to understand that this story isn't an amazingly lucky find. I started with no idea WHERE I was going to look for my treasure, and in the process of hunting, I actually came across OTHER POTENTIAL TREASURES that I could have researched. One of those is the unsigned painting that hangs in my living room, and the other is the BACHE FAMILY ALBUM. I'm not 100% convinced that this album really was destroyed in the suspicious Bristol fire.

Another wonderful example is "THE FAINTING LADY."

On January 15, 2018 "STRANGE INHERITANCE" aired a show that presented a classic example of how internet treasure hunting can uncover real treasures of extraordinary value.

In 2011, the Landau brothers inherited a number of old paintings from their father. These paintings were not considered to have any great value, so a number were stored in the family basement in their New Jersey home. No one locally knew enough about these paintings to have either the interest or the curiosity to do any research. In 2015, the brothers decided to move the old paintings out and sell them along with other inherited items, and they hired well known art auctioneer, John Nye, to handle the sale. Mr. Nye came to the house and gave his best estimate assessment of their value. One of those paintings was called "TRIPLE PORTRAIT WITH LADY FAINTING." It appeared to be UNSIGNED and was valued at about $500. Mr. Nye listed them on his auction website for two weeks before his actual live bidding auction, but even with the advance listing, there was still very little local interest. However, there were INTERNATIONAL bidders registered for the auction, which was normal in Nye&Company events.

When the auction started, the sales expectation was for a low bid of $500 and a high of $1000.

The bidding on Lot 216 "TRIPLE PORTRAIT WITH LADY FAINTING" started slowly, until it passed $1000, and then three important international phone bidders jumped in.

The price rose quickly to $10,000, much to the total shock of the auctioneer and the bidding audience.

Then up to $50,000, and then $100,000

$200,000

$300,000

$500,000

$600,000

The bidding finally topped out at $870,000, and the hammer dropped! The total price, including commission, was $1.1 million, leaving everyone stunned. Over a million dollars for a painting valued at little more than $500!

The three international bidders knew something that no one else knew. They were all EXPERTS on the earliest works of Rembrandt, and they all believed it COULD be one of his lost works called "THE UNCONSCIOUS PATIENT."

Rembrandt had painted five paintings called "the five senses" featuring the senses of touch, sight, hearing, taste and smell in 1625 when he was a teenager, and his works featuring SMELL and TASTE had been lost. These bidders were gambling that THIS could be one of those lost painting, but there was no guarantee.

The winning bidder was a French art dealer, and after he had the painting cleaned, he discovered Rembrandt's MONOGRAM disguised in a piece of furniture. This was the only one with his monogram, and his hidden monogram revealed its true provenance!

The French art dealer turned around and resold the painting for $3 million dollars to New York art collector Thomas Kaplan.

Image courtesy of John Nye/NYE&Company

This COULD have been YOU, if early Rembrandt's had been your area of expertise, and YOU had visited Mr. Nye's auction website (www.nyeandcompany.com) in the two weeks prior to the auction. This still CAN BE YOU, because Rembrandt's allegorical painting for TASTE is still missing.

34

A Ten Step Guide to Treasure Hunting on the Internet

NOW THAT YOU'VE been with me every step of the way, I'm hoping you'll be inspired to do your own treasure hunt for fortune and fame! If you ARE inspired, here are the ten steps that can get you started on your own personal treasure hunt, without ever leaving the comforts of home.

TEN STEPS FOR A SUCCESSFUL TREASURE HUNT

1. Pick a treasure category that's something you enjoy and something you're interested in. This way your search will always be fun and never work!
2. Learn as much as you can about your category as a whole. Get the leading guide book, and read it cover to cover. Follow auctions and prices, and learn what's valuable and what's not. Learn what's controversial in your category.
3. Narrow your target to those areas that interest you most and have the most value, and then narrow it again.
    By way of example:
    > Sports memorabilia narrowed to BABE RUTH, and then to AUTOGRAPHED BASEBALLS

Comic books narrowed to WALT DISNEY, and then to UNCLE SCROOGE

U.S. Coins narrowed to issues that were largely MELTED, and then to 1895 MORGAN DOLLARS

Art narrowed to OLD MASTERS, and then to EARLY REMBRANDTS

Baseball Cards narrowed to pre -1950, and then to LOU GEHRIG

Stamps narrowed to ERRORS, and then to EARLY INVERTS like the upside down train.

4. Learn as much as possible about your new narrow target. Track every example you can find that falls into your narrow target. Learn as much as possible from all the other experts. Your category will become tightly defined enough, so you can become the world's leading expert with a lot of "on line" study.

5. Become the leading expert in evaluating CONDITION for your target. In almost every category, condition is the driving force behind value. Finding items where condition is understated is ALWAYS a sure way of getting a great value.

6. Become the leading expert in evaluating the number of examples in existence. Unrecognized SCARCITY is ALWAYS a sure way of getting a great value.

7. Look for CONTROVERSIAL ITEMS. Sometimes there will be questions about the history, and even the legitimacy, of an item. THE GREATEST SINGLE WAY TO FIND VALUE IS TO PURCHASE SOMETHING THAT YOU KNOW IS REAL, BUT OTHERS HAVE DOUBTS. After purchase, you'll have to PROVE that it IS real. This will require a great deal of research, but the rewards are huge! Just consider the example of "THE FAINTING LADY!"

8. Research the HISTORY of an item. Establishing an important historical provenance is ALWAYS a sure way to increase value. Great stories will add value too. Prior ownership by famous people will also add value. It's not enough to SAY your item has a story. You'll have to PROVE the story, and PROVE the famous

ownership. This will require lots of research, just as we did on THE CINDERELLA COIN.

Anecdotal history may seem like a great story, but it isn't worth anything unless you can PROVE it's true. Remember my disappointment with the BABE RUTH autographed baseball.

9. HEDGE YOUR BET! There may be some other way to make your search pay off, other than the object itself. THE CURSE OF OAK ISLAND TV show is a way for the Lagina brothers to cover costs, even if their search is never successful. This year, they expanded their hedge, by launching a new TV series called THE CURSE OF CIVIL WAR GOLD.

If you know more about your target than anyone else, you'll see value that others don't see. You'll be able to HEDGE your bet, which can help minimize your risk , just like the Lagina brothers.

10. It usually makes the most sense to hold your acquisition for at least 5 years before reselling. There's a historic pattern of price inflation that takes place over time, and you can use this to your advantage. However, if you make an exceptional acquisition, it's possible to immediately resell at double or triple your purchase price. This is often the case when the item is controversial or "suspect," and you favorably resolve the controversy after purchase.

A FEW EXAMPLES OF HIDDEN VALUE

Did you know that there are many extremely valuable items hidden away in local historic societies that remain "undiscovered?"

Local historic societies almost never have the staff or money to search their old archives. Often, the best they can do is catalog the donation/donor, and move their gift to a storage space. Amazing treasures are being discovered every year in these local societies. It may even be possible to buy some of these hidden treasures, if the organizations need money.

Did you know that real gemstones and gold settings are often mixed in with antique costume jewelry? This isn't true for jewelry stores and on line auctions, but it IS true for great aunt Ethel's costume jewelry that's been stored in your parent's attic for the past 40 years. It's true, because semi-precious gemstones and gold weren't all that expensive in the 1920's, and gold was a very easy metal to work with. It's also true, because the people who put all of aunt Ethel's Jewelry into that box 70 years ago didn't bother to sort out the real from the "fake." They just assumed it was ALL costume jewelry. The easiest way to tell if aunt Ethel's sapphire ring is real, is to expose it to fluorescent light. A real sapphire will glow in the dark.

Did you know that some comic books are extremely rare, because poor quality paper was used in their production ? One of the rarest comic books in HIGH QUALITY condition, is the same one mentioned in the beginning of this book. UNCLE SCROOGE #6, the story of TRALLA LA published in 1954, was made using paper that disintegrated quickly. There are only 9 unrestored CGC certified copies in existence, and only 2 are graded in "very fine" condition. By comparison SUPERMAN #1, published in 1939, has 135 CGC certified copies and 9 in "very fine" or better condition. SUPERMAN #1, in that same very fine grade, sells for more than a million dollars, while the Uncle Scrooge #6 last sold for $370.

Another extreme rarity is the 1941 LARGE FEATURE COMIC #20, with only 4 certified copies known, and the best is graded at only 5.5. Very few copies survive, because it's an oversized comic book made with very poor quality paper. However, the most important reason for its rarity is that it's a comic PAINT book. The act of painting destroyed almost all the copies ever made.

Did you know that some of the rarest comic books were made as recently as 1980? In 1980 Whitman produced a number of comics that were only sold in "3 packs" (3 comics in a sealed plastic bag), and there was very limited distribution. As a result, very few of these comics exist today, and they're quite rare even though they aren't very old. As rare as THEY are, if you ever found one of those "3 packs" that was still unopened, it would be 100 times rarer than a single comic. There are probably no more than 3 or 4 unopened Whitman "3 packs" in existence today, and they're an important part of modern comic book history.

Did you know that "rarity" in collectible coins now extends beyond the actual number minted and the number still in existence? Rarity is now considered at every condition level. The New Orleans Mint made 10.7 million 1886-O MORGAN DOLLARS, and you can buy one in "fine" condition for about $30. That very same coin in uncirculated condition (MS 65) last sold for $153,000. Another example is a West Point minted 1995 proof Silver Eagle. In deep cameo proof 69 condition, this coin sells for about $6,000, but if it jumps just one point to proof 70, the price skyrockets to $43,000.

At the top of Numismatic collections are the REGISTRY SETS. A Registry set is a collection of a specific type of coin (e.g. Buffalo Nickles) that is "registered," and given an official ranking. A set of Buffalo Nickles might be ranked #10, or perhaps even #1, and that would mean it's the tenth best or first best collection in existence. There is tremendous competition among Registry set owners aspiring to move their collection higher on the Registry scale. THIS puts upward pressure on the prices for those coins that are graded as the finest known specimens.

Did you know that one of the surest ways to increase the value of an unsigned painting is to identify the artist who painted it?

A great treasure hunt opportunity is to focus on a few artists who didn't always sign their works. By becoming an expert in their style and their subject matter, you may be able to spot one of their unsigned paintings when you see it.

Did you know that the value of many pieces of pottery and art depends entirely on who made them? This can be especially difficult to determine with unsigned pieces, BUT It IS possible for experts to determine the maker through forensic analysis and style. Unsigned pottery and glass pieces can be a real opportunity, IF you're an expert. Also, most people may not know where to look for a signature if it does exist. The signature location depends on the artist and can be small and obscurely located, but if you're an expert, you'll know exactly where to look.

Did you know that in the year 2000, the U.S. Mint accidentally produced some coins with a Washington quarter front and a one dollar Sacajawea reverse? They're called "MULES." People are still finding them in circulation, and one of these "MULES" sold in March, 2018 for $192,000.

Did you know that "forgery" is rampant in virtually every collectible category? There are far more forged "Babe Ruth" autographed baseballs than there are real ones. If it's a valuable item, then someone will try to make a counterfeit and sell it. This is why there are grading and authentication companies, so buyers can avoid that risk. This also represents an opportunity. If YOU can tell the difference between a real and a counterfeit, you'd be able to buy an uncertified item at a fraction of the price. About ten years ago, a coin dealer thought he would generate a lot of interest at the Florida United Numismatists Convention by bringing the four known authentic 1913 Liberty Nickles together with one well known counterfeit. It generated more interest than he ever imagined, because the counterfeit turned out to be real! It's now worth $3.5 million, rather than nothing.

Did you know that The United States started minting coins in 1792, and the U.S. Mint made a number of "patterns" that were never meant for circulation. HERITAGE AUCTIONS sold twenty four of them over the past five years, and the AVERAGE selling price was MORE THAN $700,000 each! Finding one of these is an instant treasure!

THE ONE SECRET TO SUCCESS

When everything is said and done, there is just ONE secret to success, and that secret is KNOWLEDGE!

If you know MORE about your treasure target than anyone else, you'll be able to read the signs that others can't read, and you'll see the value that's hidden from everyone else. The treasures are out there, and "lucky" people are finding them every day. You can find them too, but you don't have to be lucky. You just have to be SMART!

Even if you NEVER find your treasure, you'll STILL WIN, because you'll become the world's leading expert in something you love, and you can carry that with you for the rest of your life.

Appendix

1838-O HALF DOLLAR RESEARCH PUBLISHED IN E-SYLUM ON OCTOBER 30, 2016

NEW RESEARCH PROVES THAT THE TYLER/BACHE SPECIMEN IS THE ONLY SURVIVING ORIGINAL 1838-O HALF DOLLAR

In January-March 2016, NGC conducted an exhaustive out of holder examination of the TYLER/BACHE 1838-O half dollar. It is one of only nine known specimens, and the purpose of this review was to determine if it had characteristics that made it different from the other eight.

SUMMARY OF RESEARCH FINDINGS

1. The Tyler/Bache specimen has the least developed GR-1 die crack on the reverse and it is therefore the earliest produced of all the known survivors.

2. The Tyler/Bache specimen has dentil distress marks on its lower reverse that were made by the loose reverse die at the end of the Jan1839 original (first) production run. This run was intended to test the large dollar press in order to make coins for circulation, but the reverse die support system collapsed after only 10 coins were struck, and it was not possible to make more at that time.

3. No other specimens have even the slightest reverse marks that could be attributable to the loose reverse die. These marks would have to be present if the others were produced in this same run because they were all struck later than Tyler/Bache and have more developed GR-1die cracks. Therefore, Tyler/Bache MUST BE THE ONLY SURVIVOR FROM THE ORIGINAL RUN.

4. The Tyler/Bache specimen has a weak/shallow strike. This weak strike is due to two factors. First, the coins in this original run were intended for circulation rather than as proofs for the Mint Director. Second, the original run had to use the dollar press because the half dollar press was not ready for production. The reverse half dollar die was too short to be secured into the larger dollar press, and Rufus Tyler, the Chief Coiner, had to splice it into place. We can infer that Tyler would have used lower striking pressure on his "jury rigged" system in an attempt to reduce the risk of failure.

   All the other specimens have very strong, sharp, strikes that are stronger than even the PROOF 1838 half dollars made in Philadelphia. We can conclude that these other specimens COULD NOT HAVE BEEN MADE ON THE DOLLAR PRESS AT A LATER DATE because their strikes are too strong.

5. All other specimens are PROOFS Produced at a later date on the half dollar press for Mint Director Patterson.

OVERALL CONCLUSION

All known 1838-O half dollars fall into two groups. They are:

ORIGINALS
- made for circulation in New Orleans in Jan 1839
- made on the dollar press
- made under lower striking pressure
- only one survivor

PROOF RESTRIKES
- made as proofs for Mint Director Patterson in New Orleans in late March/early April 1839
- made on the half dollar press
- made under higher striking pressure
- eight survivors

For the full text of the research study, please access the URL below.
https://www.dropbox.com/s/krz6uff9w9fjr3q/TYLERBACHE.pdf?dl=0

LETTER SHEDS LIGHT ON 1838-O HALF STRIKINGS

(Published in E-Sylum on June 25, 2017)

NEWLY DISCOVERED LETTER SUGGESTS A POSSIBLE 1838-O DECEPTION

On May1, 2017 a previously unknown letter from The Chief Coiner of the New Orleans Mint to New Orleans Mint Superintendent David Bradford was discovered in the National Archives, and this letter suggests that Tyler may have intentionally deceived Robert Patterson regarding 1838-O half dollar specimens sent to Philadelphia. The Tyler letter is dated April 16, 1839, and the critical portion reads as follows: "THE LARGE COINING PRESS BEING NOW IN SUCCESSFUL OPERATION WILL OF COURSE DOUBLE THE AMOUNT OF COINAGE IN BALANCE WITH THE SAME COUNT OF LABOUR."

This newly discovered letter is significant because it PROVES that the large coining press was NEVER made operational after the first "circulation strike" run of 1838-O half dollars in January 1839 and before the start up of the half dollar press on March 27, 1839. While most experts agreed that an interim repair of this large press was extremely unlikely, it always remained a possibility. This letter confirms the conclusions in "ALIGNMENT OF THE STARS" by Dannreuther and Flynn (published 2016) that there were ONLY TWO production periods for the 1838-O half dollar. The first was in Jan 1839 in New Orleans on the large dollar press to make circulation strikes per the written directive of Mint Director Patterson. This event is well documented via archival letters. Exactly 10 circulation strikes were struck before the support system for the reverse die collapsed ending the run. The second run was on March 27 in New Orleans on the half dollar press which had finally become operational. There is absolutely no documentation for this second run, but Dick Graham and John Dannreuther have proven this run took place with their examination of existing specimens.

Dick Graham is the Numismatic expert on the "Reeded Edge" half dollars which includes the 1838-O. He has identified the GR-1 reverse die crack as a key marker for ALL 9 known 1838-O and MOST 1839-O half dollars, and the extent of this crack determines the sequence in which these coins were struck. Those coins with the most developed crack were struck latest while those with the least developed crack were struck earliest.

John Dannreuther has studied most of the 1838-O and 1839-O ("Proof") half dollars and has been able to determine a sequence of production. He discovered that the Smithsonian (Mint Cabinet) specimen was produced AFTER one or more of the 1839-O "proof" half dollars. He also established that all 9 known 1838-O half dollars have less developed GR-1 die cracks than any circulation strike 1839-O's, and therefore had to have been produced before those circulation strikes. On March 29, 1839, New Orleans Mint Superintendent Bradford wrote Mint Director Patterson that Tyler had made the half dollar press operational and production of 1839-O half dollars had begun on March 27.

"I have the pleasure of informing you that Mr. Tyler has got the half dollar coining press in operation. He commenced striking on the evening of the 27th inst and the press is now performing admirably." (*courtesy National Archives Philadelphia*)

This means that the Smithsonian "proof" 1838-O MUST HAVE BEEN PRODUCED ON MARCH 27 ON THE HALF DOLLAR PRESS BEFORE THE PRODUCTION START UP OF CIRCULATION STRIKE 1839-O's. This timing makes sense because the production of proofs is "one at a time" process, while the production of circulations strikes is a continuous automatic operation. It would be extremely inefficient to interrupt the continuous striking once it had started.

In ALIGNMENT OF THE STARS, Dannreuther and Flynn also postulate that 4 or 5 other proofs may have been made at that time (since lost) in order to get closer to the currently accepted mintage total of "not more than 20" (10 circulation strikes on the first run plus 6 proofs on the second). They also postulate that these coins were requested by Mint Director Patterson for his Mint Cabinet collection. This conjecture is very reasonable given that one of these proofs is in the Mint collection.

ADDITIONAL RESEARCH AND FINDINGS

New research on one of the 1838-O half dollars was completed in 2016 and published in E-Sylum on October 30, 2016. This research PROVES (based again on GR-1 die cracks) that there is ONLY ONE SURVIVOR FROM THE FIRST CIRCULATION RUN IN JAN 1839. This means that all 8 remaining specimens had to have been produced in the second run on March 27. The research also shows that all 8 of these specimens were sent to Patterson based on their survival rate, condition and late appearance in the numismatic marketplace. The newly discovered April 16, 1839 Tyler letter proves that there was no press available to produce any of these 8 other specimens before March 27. This is an excessively large number to send to Patterson for the selection of one for his Mint Cabinet Collection, and that presumes a 100% survival from the March 27 run. The best estimate is that 10 proofs were produced on March 27 with 8 surviving to this day.

THE PATTERSON DIRECTIVE

Patterson learned of the failure of the Jan 1839 circulation strike run in a a letter from Rufus Tyler dated February 25, 1839.

"I have however spliced one of them (the reverse die) in order to try the press and succeeded in making 10 excellent impressions, the very first one struck being as perfect as the dies and entirely satisfactory, but the piece upon the bottom of the die became loose and I was unable to strike any more without fixing." (*courtesy of the National Archives Philadelphia*)

After learning of this failure, Patterson sent the following letter on March 15, 1839 to Superintendent Bradford.

"I advise that the dies of 1838 be not used by you, that we have sometimes used the dies of a particular year for a few days after its close." (*courtesy of the National Archives Philadelphia*)

This letter is remarkable in the specificity of his order. It was an absolute ban on any further use of the 1838 dies, and he did not make any exception for the production of proofs for his Mint Cabinet collection. The production and distribution (by obvious extension) of out of date coins was against his policy. He ordered that "The dies of 1838 BE NOT USED BY YOU."

The order contained in this letter was so clear that Bradford felt compelled to affirm his receipt of the directive AND that he had passed it on to Chief Coiner Rufus Tyler. At this time, letters between Philadelphia (Patterson) and New Orleans (Bradford) took about 7 to

10 days to get to their destination, so Bradford would have received the directive before the half dollar press start up on March 27. On March 29, 1839, Bradford wrote to Patterson as follows:

"I stated to Mr. Tyler that you advised that the dies of 1838 be not used and I suggested that it would be best to return them to you, thinking that they might serve some purpose, but he thought it not worthwhile." (*courtesy of the National Archives Philadelphia*)

THE FIRST PROBLEM

Given the clarity of Patterson's order that "The dies of 1838 be not used by you," the production of one or more 1838 samples for his cabinet collection would have REQUIRED another letter to Bradford making this request. Patterson would have had to reverse his previous "not used by you" order just days after it was issued, which would have been most unlikely and out of character. In addition there would have to have been considerable correspondence regarding his new order, the production of the proof samples, the shipping and finally the receipt of these samples by Patterson. As stated earlier, absolutely NO DOCUMENTATION referencing this second March 27 proof run has ever been found. The explanation that ALL the letters on this particular subject have been lost is not very credible.

THE IMPOSSIBLE PROBLEM

The second problem renders impossible the entire theory that Patterson REQUESTED any samples for his Mint Cabinet Collection. On March 29,1839 Bradford wrote to Patterson that his direct order that the dies of 1838 "be not used by you" had been given to Chief Coiner Tyler. However, WE HAVE PROVEN THAT THE PROOFS HAD ALREADY BEEN PRODUCED ON MARCH 27, 1839.

Since it is not possible (based on GR-1 die cracks) that any 1838-O's were made after that date, it is an inescapable conclusion that these 10 coins were not made AT Patterson's request. Clearly, no letter from

Patterson with a change in policy had been received by Bradford two full days AFTER the proofs had already been struck. Rather, they were made DIRECTLY AGAINST THE EXPLICIT ORDERS OF BOTH PATTERSON AND BRADFORD, AND THE COINS WERE THEN SENT TO PATTERSON BY TYLER.

THE POSSIBLE DECEPTION

THE REASON WHY THE PROHIBITED COINS MIGHT HAVE BEEN MADE

It is clear from Patterson's order that the minting of out of date coins AND THE DISTRIBUTION OF THESE COINS was against his policy. Upon receipt of this order, Bradford asked Patterson how properly to dispose of the dies. Bradford wanted to return them to Patterson, and it is highly probable that he ordered Tyler to return the coins as well. If Tyler no longer had the original circulation strikes or if he felt they were not of adequate quality to be presented to the Mint Director, he would have had a major problem. This problem would have been aggravated by the fact that he needed to be in Patterson's good graces due to his conflicts with Bradford and his pending investigation.

The only way out of this situation would have been the clandestine striking of 10 extremely high quality replacement coins to send to Patterson instead of the originals. The images below show the only surviving circulation strike and a representative "replacement" proof restrike. It is clear from these images that the replacements proofs would have presented a far superior picture of Tyler's work.

TYLER/BACHE CIRCULATION STRIKE   ELIASBERG PROOF RESTRIKE

(Images courtesy of Heritage Auction Galleries)

HOW THE PROHIBITED COINS COULD HAVE BEEN MADE

The space in the New Orleans coining area was limited, and it is clear from sworn testimony in the Tyler/Bradford investigation that others were well aware of their surroundings and took note of any "unusual" activity. How could Tyler accomplish a clandestine striking of 1838-O half dollars without drawing any attention from his co-workers? There are three unusual events that would have helped greatly in any deception. First, Tyler's production run began on the EVENING of March 27 rather than during normal working hours. Second, the production of 1839-O "proofs" has never been explained. There was no need and no request for such samples. By indicating that he was going to use the initial March 27 start up of the half dollar press to make some "test" 1839-O proofs, Tyler would have been able to conduct "single coin" production along with die and planchet polishing without raising any suspicions. Third, by retaining the 1838 reverse, even though it was cracked and he had a perfect 1839 reverse, he would have eliminated the need to switch the reverse dies, further minimizing unusual activity.

SUMMARY

WE NOW KNOW THE FOLLOWING:

1. Exactly 10 circulation 1838-O half dollars were struck in Jan 1839 on the large dollar press in New Orleans, and there is only one survivor from that run. This first circulation run was specifically ordered by Mint Director Patterson.
2. Between 8 and 10 (best estimate 10) "Proof restrikes" were made on March 27, 1839 on the half dollar press in New Orleans, and there are 8 survivors from this run. This production run was specifically prohibited by both Mint Director Patterson and Superintendent Bradford.
3. No documented evidence of this second run has ever been found, and this documentation should exist because of Patterson's explicit prohibition order.
4. The prohibited proof restrikes were sent to Mint Director Patterson.
5. There were no other production runs of 1838-O half dollars.

It is SPECULATION that the proof restrikes were made as replacements for the original circulation strikes and that this was a deception orchestrated by Tyler, but I have found it difficult to come up with any other explanation that accounts for the 5 proven facts above. As a result, I STRONGLY ENCOURAGE OTHER E-SYLUM READERS TO OFFER THEIR THOUGHTS ON THIS SUBJECT. ANY NEW EVIDENCE OR EXPLANATION IS EXTREMELY WELCOME!